ON THE ROAD

DRIVING ADVENTURES, PLEASURES AND DISCOVERIES

by Peter Schindler

dance
as though no one is watching you

love
as though you've never been hurt before

wine & dine
as though it is both the first and the last time

drive
as though heaven is on earth

ON THE ROAD

DRIVING ADVENTURES, PLEASURES AND DISCOVERIES

by Peter Schindler

To Fridl who, against my expectation,
encouraged my passion for racing and driving,

&

To Angie who, by giving me a special book
about Pininfarina, opened the flood gates to writing this book,
and has never stopped supporting me since.

CONTENTS

I have created this book to celebrate the pleasures of driving.

The stories within are about my personal journey and
discoveries, the fun I've had, and continue to have, behind the wheel.

The photographs you will see presented along the way are meant
to give you a glimpse of the many-splendoured world of driving, a
world far larger than I have yet managed to explore.

Together, the stories and photographs will, I hope, inspire you to
discover the pleasures of being on the road.

So, start your engines now…

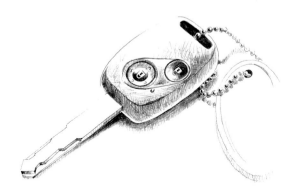

On the Road

"There is only one thing that makes a dream impossible to achieve: the fear of failure." – Paulo Coelho.

We had been driving in Brittany all day, where making cider and crêpes is an art. We bought one bottle of the cider, for memory's sake, and a cookbook, too, *Crêpes and Galettes*, to add to my wife's sprawling collection of such items.

On our return to the hotel, I found the Sunday July 4th edition of the Daily Telegraph on our room's dressing table. Splashed across the front page was Maria Sharapova's victory at Wimbledon. Since I am passionate about tennis and instantly fell in love with her looks, I picked up the paper and began to read. She had beaten Serena Williams, 6-1, 6-4, it said. She was a 17-year-old Russian and the lowest seed ever to win on the Centre Court, it continued. "A Star is Born" is what the article didn't say, but had written all over it. It made me think nostalgically of beauty, youth, talent, energy and boundless opportunity, and what all that could mean.

Not that I was ever good-looking, but there was a time when I had youth, energy and maybe even talent. I had certainly felt so on the day that a motor sport magazine had published an article about a race I had won with the title "A Star is Born". Not that the win on that day could in the least be compared with Maria's achievement – don't I wish I was on a first-name basis with her - but, looking back, I can't help but feel that I was on to something precious and threw it away. It was all too difficult, I used to say. What if success never comes? What if I fail? Yes, what if?

Not that I've led a miserable life since then, far from it, but I've wondered on more than a few occasions what could have been if I had taken the star that was supposedly born and made it rise. What if? I'm not sure if you can relate, but it's a feeling I always thought I could do without.

So, I don't know what it was – the cider or the crêpes? – on the day I read the article about Ms. Sharapova, but it hit me like a thunderbolt: forget about "What if?"! It's never too late.

After all, ever since the time I had raced full of hope, I have never once failed to enjoy myself driving, at any time of day, in any season, on any kind of surface – hot or wet tarmac, gravel, and especially snow – and in any country. In fact, I've had some of the best times of my life on the road. Some pleasures have gone, others may have changed, yet others I've discovered along the way. My passion for driving is as hot as ever.

Driving has made me feel free and relaxed, and able to live life to the fullest. When I drive on an open road toward the horizon, I quickly forget my daily worries; the distance beckons me with the promise of something new, different and previously unexplored. By giving me the choice to turn left or right, to go straight or to stop for a rest, driving puts me in control, as I rarely am, and makes me unencumbered and adventurous.

Driving quenches my thirst for motion, no less than when I ski, skate, or surf and my body leans and bends to maintain balance – but in far more comfortable, safe and indulgent surroundings. This gets to the heart of my driving pleasure: I can observe life and participate in it, both at the same time.

The driving experience also stimulates my senses. The touch of wind as it tousles and whips my hair, the sense of romance as I curve along an ocean road and the nervous excitement as I twist along narrow Alpine roads, the sight of magnificent vistas and amazing cloud formations, the smell of pastures, meadows and forests as I drive by. Not to mention the in-car experience of a stylish cabriolet redolent with the smell of its interior trimmings, embraced by curvaceous seats and the rich sounds of the CD player throbbing with my favourite on-the-road music. All these combine to make me feel special and indulged and have not changed an iota since I first hit the road.

The obsession with speed and the search for a perfect car have come and gone, now well replaced by new pleasures discovered along the way. For example, I've come to experience the satisfaction of manual labour as when I had to push or pull my car out from one ditch or another. Through driving, I have even found myself; I've learned what makes me tick, what fills me with bliss. Not only that, I now know that I can bring about this state of bliss at just about any time. So long as there is a car and an open road, I can be at one with myself. I've turned strangers into friends on the road and had the pleasure of meeting people who know how to make much of little. Conversely, because of my encounters with people on the road, I've realised that the smaller the differences among us, the larger they tend to loom. I've learned about the cultures of other countries, merely by virtue of driving there. Driving for thousands of miles with my future wife also proved an invaluable test of our suitability for marriage. Now, when we have a disagreement, we know that all we need to do to put things right is either get on the road, or get naked. Neither is a disagreeable choice.

What I realised while holding the Sunday Telegraph in my hands, is that even though I had given up racing eons ago, I had never really stopped loving driving, and that there are different ways to celebrate the pleasures of being on the road. All I had done is to take a detour, and this is where most of the interesting things in life happen anyway. Being on the

road has been an adventure and the source of immense pleasure, again and again. Bearing in mind that memory is a poor guide to the past, here are the most memorable milestones along the journey: when I was in my late teens, my relentless pursuit of acrobatics on snow and my lusting after sheer speed; my infatuation with cars; my love affair with roads; the realisation that fulfilment in life depends on what we make out of it; the making of friends; the making of a shared life; the discoveries of foreign cultures; and, at last, the celebration of how lovely it is to feel free and unencumbered. All this merely by spending a lot of time on the road. Not bad, especially since it also is a fair approximation to my progression in life.

Bon voyage!

3. February 2005

CHAPTER ONE

Abandon

"Youth would be an ideal state if it came a little later in life."
– Lord Asquith.

M ost of us begin driving during our late teens, at an age when, with hindsight, we know that restraint is desirable, but as difficult to impart to the adolescent as to the cork of an excited bottle of champagne in the heat of summer. It is an age of wild enthusiasm for life and adventure, for breaking loose, and for exploding the shackles of the parental grip.

That's how it was for me. Cars and driving have been with me for as long as I can remember. At the age of four or thereabouts, I spent countless hours playing with my toy cars making mock-realistic engine noises and riding my tricycle on two wheels around the tables and chairs under our pergola, again and again, and again.

As I grew older, I played with real cars on private property, producing the occasional dent but without denting my own enthusiasm and craving for driving. On my 18th birthday – not a day later – I picked up my driving licence. The wait was over; I was free at last. It was ten years since I had first dreamt of being allowed to drive on my own; the wait had seemed interminable. That Wednesday in February, the dawn of the day I had craved for a long decade, the moment for me to get in my rinky-dink little car that meant everything to me eventually arrived. In the event, it was a cloudy, even dreary winter day. Yet nothing could cloud my joy, nothing impede the fulfilment of my anticipation. For me, it was the brightest day yet in my life. The instant I drove off in my used Renault 5GL (christened "Kermit" because it was as green as the eponymous creature), for the first time unaccompanied and with no purpose other than to drive, a door opened. I stepped into my free world and headlong into two obsessions. One was and still is the world of snow; the other was but is no longer that of speed.

* * *

I don't recall whether I became enamoured with snow because I was born in February and hence obtained my driving licence in winter or because I grew up on skis. At any rate, I've loved driving on snow for as long as I can remember. While perhaps you can appreciate the desire to seek speed for speed's sake, especially in the heat of summer, understanding why anyone would be fascinated with driving in winter and on snow may be a bit harder. After all, isn't driving in winter dreadful? You get stuck in traffic, no? Your hands get frostbitten every morning trying to scrape clear a few peep-holes so you can see, right? Cars fail to start and door locks are frozen shut. How much fun is that? But for me, driving on snow in a pristine winter landscape holds the same attraction as skiing on fresh powder, half-immersed, half-floating, leaning back, swinging from side to side, into the sun, ever downhill. Driving has always been more akin to a hobby than a mode of transportation.

The pleasure of driving on snow started the day I got my driving licence. When I wasn't pursuing Renault 5GL speed records on German highways, I took my Kermit onto wintry Alpine roads from the very first day, because, quite simply, it was both a challenge as well as immense fun. Many times, especially in the midst of dense snowfall, I went out for a drive in the middle of the night, always equipped with a shovel, often also with an intrepid friend. Night time was perfect, because it felt safe. At night, there wasn't much traffic and what on-coming cars there were, one could see from afar because of their headlights. (The fact that a broken-down car could have been lurking, invisibly, around the next corner and presented me with an unavoidable obstacle was simply lost on me at that time.)

And so, I took to the wintry roads night after night and relished sliding through the bends in the fluffy surroundings of soft snow. I learned, after repeated attempts, how to slow down as straight and as quickly as possible, not with the help of modern ABS, but by stutter-braking (on, off, on, off the brake as rapidly as my young feet made it possible). I learned how to bring the back of Kermit around when its front was intent on going straight by pulling the parking brake for a split second to lock its rear wheels. I learned how to bring its rear-end back in line when it threatened to break into a spin by counter-steering and, for heaven's sake, keeping my foot on the gas.

More than once I left the road involuntarily, of course. I recall one particularly memorable event when I first lost traction, and then my mind. My friend and I were on one of our nightly outings when I lost it on a turn and poor Kermit ended up in a ditch, not far from the road. I couldn't back it out; the wheels only spun wildly in a futile attempt to find traction. So, my friend got out and started pushing, matching my rhythm as I worked the gas and the clutch. Kermit sort of worked itself into a lather, but in the end remained stuck. What to do? This was when my friend had a stroke of genius: if we both pushed, Kermit might be freed in the end. Better still if its wheels were turning in reverse at the same time. How could we achieve that? My friend had yet another brilliant idea. What if we loaded the bag of snow chains on the gas pedal? No sooner had he suggested the idea than we put it into practice. First, I put Kermit into reverse. Second, I heaved the immensely heavy bag

> "Kermit howled, snow **flew** into the air and a few seconds later, Kermit was free."

of chains onto my right foot, which was depressing the gas pedal. In one fell swoop I then pulled my foot out, leaving the bag's weight to hold the gas pedal down, jumped out and rushed to the front of the car to help my friend push. Kermit howled, snow flew into the air and a few seconds later Kermit was free. That was the good news. The bad news was that Kermit kept going. What happened next I don't quite recall, because both of us fell forward as Kermit slipped away. I do know that it took us another hour to dig Kermit out of another ditch on the other side of the road.

Today, many years later, I still enjoy driving on snow, because it requires a light touch, not a crudeness of approach. I relish it because on snow I can be playful in my car, I can move with it and it with me. It feels exhilarating because it gives me the magical feeling of floating on air, but without the need to be moving at high speed.

Oddly, driving on snow, for pleasure, feels entirely safe. In deep winter, soft snow cradles me. The surfaces are smooth and the landscape is reminiscent of a fairy tale. On the road, I see dancing flakes of snow and icing sugar-coated houses, hills and trees. All I hear is soothing silence, the silence of light feet brushing against velvet carpeting.

Before long, and as winter carries on, I often forget, even today, what it is like to be gripped by dry, clutching tarmac and begin to wonder how I can ever enjoy myself on anything but slippery surfaces. I even feel a sense of deprivation when spring returns, snow melts and the roads return to me their commanding grip. Every winter, driving on snow becomes as natural as breathing air.

* * *

"Like skiing on **fresh** powder
half-immersed, half-floating, swinging from side to side..."

My obsession with snow was benign. Not so my obsession with speed: it was malignant. Any road that I entered was there for only one purpose, namely to go as fast as possible, all the time, or so I recall. This obsession led me to view slower cars in only one of two ways: obstacles to be removed or challenges to be overcome. Either way, other cars represented a serious infraction of my freedom of expression, of my freedom to attain speed. And how I lusted after speed! Whenever I could, I would bound forward like a puppy after a thrown stick, yelping, jumping, drooling, tail wagging, except I didn't even need the stick. An open road was all that I needed.

Was there any sensible reason for it? Adults, as adults do, were trying to be helpful by asking meaningful questions: "But you're hardly gaining any time, now are you? So why drive so fast?" That didn't cut mustard with me because, obviously, they really didn't get it. The point of driving fast had never had anything to do with being in a hurry or gaining time. After all, I had nowhere to go, so what would be the point of getting there sooner? The point of driving fast was simply the joy of driving as fast as the car would permit. Period. It didn't make any sense, of course, but youth – mine anyway – had its own logic.

That almost unquenchable thirst for speed was also at the root of me having severe problems with speed limits. Not with speed limits themselves, actually, only with their unannounced enforcement. This was why I applauded those countries where politeness or the constitution required that law enforcers announce their intent: "Speed camera ahead!" I always liked that.

Better yet was driving in Germany where, on highways, there was no speed limit. Today pedal-to-the-metal speed means very little to me – the thought of speed ovals or drag racing makes me cringe, because the one reminds me of the wheels of psychotic hamsters and the other of sperm in search of a life – but at age eighteen it was a different matter. Excitedly I headed to Germany because I could drive as fast as I wanted. This was rather silly because Kermit didn't go any faster than 140kmh, if there was tail wind, the road was going downhill and we were on our way home. Even in Austria I could have done a 140kmh without the meanest gendarme finding grounds to object, but they would have had grounds to book me for intimidating other drivers by practically sitting in their luggage compartment. In Germany, you see, that wasn't a problem because even the slowest driver in the slowest car was going faster than me and my panting Kermit ever could.

So I would head across the border to a stretch of road between Memmingen and Ulm in southern Germany that is pretty much straight for thirty-seven kilometres. Whether in bright sunshine or under ominous clouds of rain, it was definitely my highway. Even today, I find that this stretch of road can mean highway driving at its best. It is largely straight, but interrupted by long, shapely bends that prevent the boredom of roads that are straight and nothing but straight. The landscape is ideal because it is beautiful, but not in an attention-grabbing sort of way. Instead, the landscape is soothing as it rushes by. The stately trees and chequered fields – fine detail that gives them grace when I see them at rest – take on the

fluid beauty of diffuse silhouettes of landscape in motion. Not that I noticed a thing about the landscape. All I recall is that it was perfect for pushing Kermit to 141kmh, maybe even 141.5kmh. I also recall regretting that the speedometer dial wasn't particularly detailed when it came to anything above 120kmh. Telling the difference between 141kmh and 141.5kmh an hour was a real strain on my eyes.

In the pursuit of speed, life also presented me with a number of difficult decisions. For example, should I save money to buy wider rims and tyres for Kermit? Yes or no? In favour was that such tyres and rims would allow me to go faster around bends. Against was the drag these would represent on achieving 141.5kmh. What to do? Easier to deal with was the question of whether to lower the car – make it more ground-hugging, in other words – because this would let me go faster through turns by virtue of Kermit's centre of gravity being lower and faster on the straights because of less air resistance. So, this was a must-do conversion. (This same logic doesn't work for people, by the way. Although you're harder to push over when you squat, you certainly can't run faster.) Turning off the ventilation fan while trying to reach top speed was also an easy decision to make (even if it meant that I would be roasting inside) since turning off the fan meant saving 0.5 horsepower, which would otherwise have gone to driving the generator when instead it could go into a bit of extra propulsion. Turning off the headlights at night would have had a similar effect, but, thank heavens, I was too scared for that.

* * *

As I reflect on those days, I realise that a lot has changed. Most significantly, my obsession with speed has waned. That's not because the fizz has gone out of the bottle; it's just that I've stopped shaking it before consumption. On the path toward a more balanced view of driving pleasure, I still had to get past another obsession, however, namely that of being unfailingly aroused and fulfilled by the allure of a beautiful car.

"Like floating
on air
but without the need to be moving at high speed..."

For once not the red-line hiss,
but a **soft purr** and
light feet on velvet carpeting...

"The stately trees take on the **fluid beauty** of diffuse silhouettes of landscape in motion..."

CHAPTER TWO

Indulgence

"Man is in love and loves what vanishes. What more is there to say?"
– W.B. Yeats.

Where would you say a frustrated race car driver from an Alpine republic – with a terminal addiction to sliding on snow – should wind up? In fact, there is only one place, and that place is Hong Kong.

Having been denied the chance to rake in prize and sponsorship dollars or to find meaningful love among the adoring groupies, Hong Kong was the place to go. It was a place to make money more readily than anywhere else. It was also a place to find silky oriental love. Plus it had mountains with grand-sounding names such as Victoria Peak – a molehill by any other name that has never once made the acquaintance of snow. Still, the presence of hills soothed my nostalgia.

Within a few years I had made good and it was time to give in to my yearning: I bought myself a beautiful new car. And where did I park it? In Europe, of course. There were two reasons for this. First, my savings didn't go far enough to be able to afford what I wanted in Hong Kong where taxes more than doubled the price of a new car. Second, I didn't see the point of owning a beautiful, fast car in a place whose roads are short, congested or both.

And so it came to pass that my new car and I had to endure a long-distance relationship. While I lived in Hong Kong, it bunked, batteries disconnected, in my parents' home in Austria. Whenever I could, I would stop by, either to renew our vows – a driving holiday – or simply for an amorous encounter to keep our relationship as fresh as on the first day. That was the plan. But it didn't work out that way. For almost one whole year after I acquired my playmate, circumstances conspired to prevent me from being able to pay a visit.

Now, distance and time make the heart grow fonder. In my case, they also led to an inexplicable urge to want to clean and cuddle my car just as soon as I would find a chance to haul myself to Europe. Rather odd, that, the longing to clean my car, I recall musing, since I had already convinced myself that the one thing that I would miss more than anything else if I ever left Hong Kong was my domestic helper, a luxury I had acquired almost as soon as I cottoned on to the fact that everyone else had one too. How wonderful was her cooking! And, more to the point, how wonderful it was not to have to clean a thing – not dishes, not clothes, not floors! So why on earth did I look forward to washing my car? I really don't know.

After eleven months, I was finally able to sneak off to Austria. I was filled to the brim with desire. So strong was the longing that even today I recall the emotional intensity of the encounter: it was about all the carnal pleasures that a mere car had the power to bestow on a warped car lover. And so, on a beautiful Saturday morning in early June, I went to work.

The mossy terra-cotta tiles in front of my parents' garage, where the grooming took place, was an idyllic place. The two patches of lawn that flanked my work area were sprinkled with blossoms and shreds of white bark from two melancholy birch trees. The leaves and branches of the birches and a giant oak tree threw sharp, swaying shadows all about me and my car. Across the work area snaked a bright-yellow water hose, and various cleaning aids were neatly lined up by the side: cleaners for windows, leather, plastic, and rubber; vacuum cleaner with special attachments; cloths, sponges, brushes. Think of the place like an outdoor beauty parlour with an assortment of money-no-object cosmetics. Never mind that the object in question was a car.

I started the ceremony by hosing my car down with the spray of a fine nozzle. I proceeded to scrub it gently with a soft sponge. Then I gave it another dousing to leave it covered with drooping pearls of clear water, which enveloped it with that indescribable freshness of a meadow in morning dew. Later, I leathered it down and applied a coating of wax, which I polished off, feeling my car's shape with hands longing to touch. If seeing is believing, then touching is belief made real.

Every now and then, I stepped back and contorted myself into an impossible position to focus on a spot at just the right angle. "Ah, I knew it, there you are!" I was talking to a leftover smudge. Immediately I was filled with a bizarre sense of satisfaction, as if each remaining smudge had been the last piece in a puzzle. Having found a smudge, I braced myself to remove it; some of these buggers clung on for their lives. Then I went on to hunt for another.

After finishing cleaning the outside of my car, I walked away from it and into full shade. My head wanted to turn as I gained distance, but I said, no, not yet, just a few more steps. Now I could look. It reminded me also of the many times when I had parked my car to go on an errand. Instead of just walking off, I couldn't help but look back to sneak a glimpse, which would fill me with pride in owning a beautiful thing. At the same time, I will readily admit, I felt totally embarrassed that I should be so much in the thrall of a mere object. After all, I was in my thirties then, old in other words, and what was my beautiful car, but a few hundred quid worth of glass, rubber, plastic, metals (some precious, some base) and, since I was lucky, fine leather? Yet, I was then, and am still today, a sucker for a beautiful thing, whether it is a human body, a cloth worked into fashion, or an elaborate decanter.

Then, as now, I felt that some cars are works of art, veritable "sculptures in motion", as Arthur Drexler, the curator at New York's Museum of Modern Arts called the Cisitalia 202 in the 1950s. But a car didn't have to be a work of art. On occasion a car endeared itself to me for the littlest thing – it might be how its colour played with light, the smooth chromium of its propped-up headlights, the arching shape of its bonnet, the sparkle of its eyes, whatever – and I latched on. What's more, it was quite likely that this one tiny part would, over time, come to reflect the dreams made possible by the whole.

But beautiful cars — and clothes, if not decanters — always did more than just tickle my sense of beauty. Their beauty also rubbed off on me, or so I always fooled myself into believing. When I sit in a gorgeous cabriolet and wrap it around me like a silken shawl, voila, aren't I the handsomest bloke there ever was! So, I resolved even then that if I ever felt the need, I would save the expense of botox treatment and instead spend my buck on yet another car. It's a better investment, I figured, not least because botox wears off with age while a car's patina will add to its and my glow over time.

While I stood back in the shade, gazing at my car, I dwelled on one more thought. As

"...which enveloped it
with that undescribable
freshness
of a **meadow**
in morning dew."

"On occasion a car endeared itself to me for

the littlest
things..."

beautiful as my car looked standing there, with light performing a shadow dance on its surface, cars are designed for motion. There is a hidden aspect of their beauty that only emerges when I see them being driven. No matter how pleasing my car was when at rest, it never looked as gorgeous as when I saw it being driven, when it would bring motion to life. It always left me without a doubt: beautiful cars are never meant to stand still.

After gazing at my car for a while, I took a few steps forward to pick up a set of dry cloths, suitable for cleaning the interior. Getting closer, I noticed for the first time during the morning's cleaning the strong smells of my car. While washing it, the dominant smell was always of soap and wet grass. But then, when my car was standing there in the nude with no adulterating scents, it enveloped me in all its fumes of oil and gas, rubber and combustion, and paint. These odours shouldn't have been appealing, but the world of smell is full of surprises. I've always been at once repulsed and attracted by the oddest of smells. The pungency of onions sends me weeping, yet makes me want to catch a whiff. The smokiness of cigars sends my head spinning, yet draws me near. Wet dogs, fishy harbour-sides, acrid hot springs, sweet-stinging alcohols, they all should, by logic, repel, not woo me. And yet they do, for reasons that are difficult to understand, except that they send me strong signs of life. That explains why I found my car's fumes so appealing: they signalled the presence of a near-human artefact that breathed, sweated, consumed and discharged as it lived.

One step closer still. I opened the door and noticed a lot of things. The windows needed cleaning. So did the door sills. The carpets were a mess. But above all, there was an invitation to leave the outside world behind. I knew I needed and wanted to continue cleaning, but for a moment, only a moment, I just got in, closed the door, sat back and took a deep breath. At once the redolence of my car's interior cradled me in comfort and signalled a very special place. It was a private place, a place I could call my own, more so than almost any other place. I felt that I was the master of this tiny universe, a universe in which I could make it so, whatever it was.

I sat in my car for a minute or two, or even more. I felt as relaxed as if I were being hugged by a friend. It couldn't be, or could it? My mind wandered to the story of M.

M has loved driving for as long as she can remember. She started driving during the war, and has fond memories of many cars. In the early days, she drove her husband's Mustard Tin, a 1929 Rolls Royce Phantom I. (The 1929 spec sheet of that car didn't give a number in the 'horse power' entry. No, it just said "adequate". Those were the days!) She was Mustard Tin because she was painted yellow, as bright as that of Coleman's mustard, all yellow, except her roof and gorgeous mudguards, which were black. And then there was a quirky Deux Chevaux, a trusty Mini and her soft-top MG Sports, emerald green with tan interior. "Oh, was she beautiful!" But the car that really stands out in her memory is a humble Ford Fiesta Ghia, which became part of M's family. In fact, it became one of her children when one day her two boys, James and Robert, at first silently and then boisterously pronounced the Fiesta's licence plate "G 137 MAH": "Gee, Ma, it really is yours!"

"It became one of her children when one day her two boys pronounced the Fiesta's license plate…"

Today G MAH is no more, and neither is Mustard Tin. But M continues to love driving. With a St. Christopher in her car, she still goes on long journeys and talks to her car about the scenery, where they are going and other drivers. "Dear Heavens, what I have seen in my time…" I recall her saying.

"Aren't cars he's?" I once asked M.

"Oh dear no!" she replied. "They are not. All my cars were shes!"

I had to admit that cars always had the power to entice me, too, into near-human relationships. I realise that this probably says more about my defective mind than you'd want to know, but still, that is quite a feat. After all, remember, cars are only a few hundred quid worth of glass, rubber, plastic, metals, and, if we're lucky, fine leather. As I washed my beautiful car, I thought back to the car to which I had been closest, that plump Renault 5GL ("Grand Luxe" no less), which was driven to speed record after speed record. That relationship started out with our positions clearly defined. I was the owner; it was the subject. As such, I recall that it had to endure a range of indignities, especially in the early days. I kicked and cursed it when it failed to start, in particular on one day when I was late, way late, for an all-important date. Nothing could move it, however. I couldn't believe it. But instead of accepting that things just happen, I attributed its behaviour to free will. It was obvious that it didn't start out of spite. How else to make sense of the fact that it wouldn't budge at such a critical moment in my life? I figured it was simply jealous. So, I kicked it and cursed it some more.

As my subject, it also had to bear witness to my opinions. I made it wear bumper stickers that expressed my mood at the time "So many pedestrians. So little time!" It accepted stoically that it was used as a billboard because at the same time it rose in status with me giving it its name: Kermit. It was Kermit, remember, because it was as bright green as that frog. Plus, I forgot to mention, it was French.

Somehow, giving my car a name prompted a change in my demeanour. The beatings became fewer. Even the opinionated stickers came off. Their place was taken, first, by a modicum of sympathy in the face of untoward events – like when it was scratched after a rough night out – and, later, by genuine caring. I even bought it mudguards, but no St.

"I was the master of this tiny universe…"

Christopher. Physical protection, I thought, was good enough.

Over time, sympathy and caring grew into attachment when I began to personalise my Kermit with stripes, a new tail pipe that would, guaranteed, add an extra 1.5 to the 43 horsepower that was standard, fog lights, a coin holder, and a CB radio with a gigantic antenna. (The antenna was bought after a lot of deliberation: after all, it meant additional air resistance.) There even came a time when I would sit in my Kermit, not to go for a drive, but to be alone and talk to myself. Kermit was the perfect sanctuary for that. And, in moments that bordered on hallucination, I swear that, like a good friend, it had an answer for all of my life's questions.

* * *

After a while, I awoke from the trance of fond memories, opened again the door of my car and refocused my mind on the task of cleaning. First, I delved into every corner of my car's interior with the vacuum cleaner's special attachment, a narrow nozzle that could penetrate even the tiniest of crevices, to remove dust, hair, and crumbs of various kinds. Next, I was ready to attend to the cleaning of the windows. Ah, the windows! How to get them clean? This, aside from the nooks and crannies of the wheels, was the biggest challenge. What worked best, I had found, was not cloth or leather or cotton puffs, but good old-fashioned broadsheet newspaper. Spray on a film of window cleaner, crumple the sheets of newspaper into a ball, and then rub the windows dry with sweeping motions.

"It cost nothing unless one bought the newspaper only for cleaning, which I was apt to do."

It would leave almost no streaks, and cost nothing, unless one bought the newspaper only for cleaning, which I was apt to do. Cleaning windows perfectly required concentration and was also a good workout because I had to apply force while bending into impossible positions.

After finishing cleaning the interior, I got back out and walked around. I wore the studious look of a police inspector: had I missed a trace of dirt? After a few minutes of focused inspection, I concluded that the job was done. My car was spanking clean, while I was a pile of dirt.

By then it was almost noon. I recall dying to go for a drive right after lunch. In order to keep my car cool for the afternoon's outing, I backed it into the garage. Seeing how dirty I was, especially my shoes, I hesitated for a second, but then came to my senses. For heaven's sake, it was only a car, no matter how beautiful or how perfect.

I got in and turned on the engine. As it sprang to life, I felt that it was making music of sorts. Had I lost my wits? Had the withdrawal symptoms been having permanent effects? It seemed, at least for a moment, that the interaction of my car's hundreds of mechanical parts – pistons, valves, cam and crank shafts, gears, fans and belts, each with its own distinct sound – generated pleasing dissonances. I listened carefully, revved it up a bit, closed my eyes and, I kid you not, picked up the sounds of trumpets, drums, cymbals, triangles, and whips. Of course, it wasn't quite as grand a lesson in music as Britten's Young Person's Guide to the Orchestra, I admit, but immensely pleasing nonetheless.

What was stronger still was the evocation of the sounds and power of elegant big cats. Their majestic power was always something I aspired to because it hinted at perfect motion, supple, graceful, and explosive. The big cats can be at rest one second, at full speed the next, turning, ducking, flying on any terrain. They are as responsive as I could only dream of being in my car. No wonder my car's sounds created an unquenchable aspiration. In fact, they were so bewitching that they became an addictive thrill. And so, I would often find myself turning down the window in tunnels, narrow alleys and steep valleys for no reason other than to revel in the pleasure of the engine's intoxicating sounds.

But that – listening intently to the sounds of my car's engine – that was for the afternoon drive. I engaged reverse and backed my car slowly into the cool stone garage, turned off the engine, closed the door and walked back out. As before, I turned around once more before I headed indoors for lunch. The impression that lingered was one of complete and utter aesthetic satisfaction.

* * *

So, my car, my Ten, appealed strongly to my senses. Great! For all that, it might have been a pair of Gucci's. Wasn't there something else?

More than an object of beauty, my car let me drive to the fullest, just as I had always wanted to live life: "Life is not a journey to the grave with the intention of arriving safely in a pretty and well-preserved body, but rather to skid in broadside, thoroughly used up, totally worn out and loudly proclaiming: 'Wow, what a ride!'"

It was a car that fit me like a glove. If it had been too loose, like ski or skate boots two sizes too big for my feet, I simply couldn't have driven it. It also gave me all-round clear vision, let me feel all the forces that acted on it and relayed, in turn, my actions – shifting gears, and working the pedals and steering wheel – at once and faithfully to its engine, brakes, wheels and gearbox.

Talking about the gearbox, I had a violent reaction to automatics. I would have never bought a car with anything but a manual gearbox because, I was adamant, that driving

"At rest one second, at full speed the next,
turning, ducking,
flying on any terrain."

pleasure came from being seriously involved, which meant, above all, feeling at one with my car. In this respect the gear stick played a vital role because it connected me to my car. It wasn't that an automatic transmission wouldn't have involved me; it was just that a manual involved me infinitely more.

(In order to leave no doubt in your mind that I was a flawed individual not only then, I now have another pet peeve: it is that many pure sports cars, e.g., over 80 percent of Ferraris, are sold with an F1-style paddle shifter. Why is this a pet peeve? Because the F1-style paddle shifter's main purpose in life is to eke out split seconds while seriously, dead-seriously, racing on a track.   Now, how many of all those Ferraris will ever be taken on a track in this way? Exactly 1%, I would say. What about the other 99 out of a 100? They are bought and parked, rarely driven, by wanna-be cool guys. Yikes!)

My perfect car was a manual, of course, and therefore felt as if it could read my mind, as if it could be steered, like a bicycle, by leaning alone. In fact, it felt as if it had become an extension of myself. It was a car that made me say, "Wow, what a ride!" no matter where we went.

It was a match made in heaven, is what it was. I felt so smug about it that I contemptuously looked down upon any other form of transportation. I sniggered about cars that were soft and wobbly. How could anyone drive such noodles? Yes, that's right! Noodle cars! In noodle cars, when I accelerate, I hear and feel the engine working well before I sense a shove, if ever it comes. More likely, I lean forward to balance the impending thrust, but wind up disappointed and dangling like a spinster's boobs in their oversized bra or, if you prefer, like her unrequited lover's jimmy in his boxers. Also, when I brake hard, noodle cars, instead of slowing down, appear to slip away from under me, as if I'd just stepped on a banana skin. But then again, what would you expect from a noodle? Push one, and it curls up; pull one, and it twists, contorts and winds up sulking in a knot. Pleasurable driving it is not.

As I am thinking back about how passionately I dismissed noodles at that time, it suddenly hits me: *Kermit was a noodle!* Ouch, this hurts. It never once behaved as I wanted. It went straight when I wanted to go around a bend. It wobbled, was rarely sure-footed, and as for fitting me like a glove, yes, like an asbestos kitchen glove on the hand of a toddler. It was faulty to a fault. So, what had happened throughout my twenties and early thirties? Was lusting after and buying Ten really all that it was cracked up to be? It couldn't be, for my Kermit was about as imperfect a car as there was, yet I loved it, deeply, despite it being French. Perhaps Ten was only perfect for a moment in my life. Perhaps there was something else. But what was it?

* * *

After lunch and finishing a double-espresso, what was on my mind then was to take my beautiful car on an adventure.

The garage door was still wide open and I got into the car that I wore like a jewel. I pulled the cabin door towards me and it fell into its lock with a sonorous thud. All was quiet then. I inhaled, deeply, and held my breath for a few seconds in utter silence.

I didn't know it, but I was perspiring. I was in a state of acute anticipation. Any moment now I would be on the road. But not just yet, because I was where I always wanted to be, where the anticipation of things to come was so strong that anticipation itself begged to go on forever.

Alright, then. I turn the key in the ignition to the right and wriggle in my seat. In the centre of the centre console a button illuminates and glows enticingly in red. It dominates my vision and defies all reason. For a brief moment it becomes the very symbol of my heart-stopping anticipation to drive and be free. "Touch me, and you won't regret it" it suggests and continues to glow.

And so I reach out. There is firm resistance to my touch, as if it means to say, don't be shy. For a half-second, maybe less, there is nothing. My heart sinks, but then, there it is. Frozen, rigid steel erupts into gushing, liquid metal. A bass growl bursts forth, then lengthens into a hiss. After a few seconds, it settles into a purr. Twelve cylinders had just fired up. The rev counter jumped from naught to 1,800 and then drew back to a steady 850.   And my state of nervous anticipation had burst free. After a few seconds, I managed to gather myself. Filled with lustful determination, I at last pulled out onto the road.

Soon it will be
spring.

CHAPTER THREE

In Motion

"Man must choose whether to be rich in things or in the freedom to use them."
– Ivan Illich.

Cars that are parked, even perfect ones, are like notes on a sheet of paper: the silence is deafening. That's why, over the years, I've come to wash my automotive possessions a lot less and, instead, drive them a whole lot more. Now, it wasn't that one day I woke up with the thought, "Who cares about cars?! It's driving that I really love!" Nah, it was a slow transformation that had, in a way, no beginning and no end. And yet, I do recall one particular drive, in a rental car no less, which marked a turning point of sorts. This drive took me onto roads in the Alps with which I was intimately familiar – I had been careening around on them since the days of Kermit – yet the experience on that day could not have been more different to all that had gone before. It was one of complete fulfilment rather than blind intoxication by virtue of racing at speed or having had my reason taken away by, you know, a few hundred quid worth of glass, rubber, plastic, metals and, if lucky, fine leather.

* * *

It was late morning when I stopped for a break. About a half-hour earlier, I had bought a light snack – freshly baked, crusty buns stuffed with aromatic salami, as only the Italians know how to make, a handful of ripe cherries and a bottle of mineral water. I vividly recall sitting on a rugged, wooden roadside bench, leaning against a fixed picnic table, all the better to soak up the sun's warm rays, smell the scents of autumn and gaze into the deep-azure sky. Even though I was no longer moving, I was still on cloud nine, breathing deeply and audibly. Since early in the morning on this spectacular October Sunday I had been chasing mountain after mountain, surging and plunging in rapid succession in the midst of Alpine splendour. The last pass we had climbed was the Timmelsjoch, the highest crossing between Austria and Italy. Only minutes ago we had stopped to take this break near St. Leonhard, which marks the end of the pass's steep descent into Italy. Even though my companion was topless and should have been feeling chilly in the cool air of the shade, she, too, was still showing signs of excitement: she crackled and made the air over her bonnet shimmer. Looking at her body reflecting the glorious landscape, I completely forgot that only twenty-four hours earlier I had bitched and moaned about the mix-up that had left me driving a rental when I could have had one of my amorous encounters with my gorgeous car. Instead of being preoccupied with frustration, however, I was flush with the relish that came from the sheer pleasure of driving, a pleasure I had rarely, if ever, felt so intensely, and so differently. I remember saying to myself as I was resting by the roadside on that day, "Oh my, how things have changed!"

The drive had started early in the morning, very early. Even though all my friends would say that I am – and always have been – one of those incomprehensible morning people, the

"The drive had started early in the morning."

truth is I hate being woken up by an alarm clock as much as anyone else. In fact, if I could have one wish in my life come true, it would be the disinvention of these hideous devices.

But on days when I have the luxury of driving for pleasure, then the agony of waking to the sound of an alarm clock in what is practically the middle of the night, is almost instantaneously replaced with wanton anticipation of the treat to come. In no time, I am up, dressed, have put on my soft running shoes, all the better to work the pedals, and rushed out to my car. This much has not changed, and I don't think ever will.

At any rate, on that day I was starting off in Bregenz, an Austrian town by Lake Constance. Even though I had only my rental, I was determined not to let that fact get in the way. After all, I had a free day on my hands, plus I hadn't been driving for a while, so, without question, I would spend it out on the road. Also, the car I had rented was, by most standards, quite an object of desire.

At first, with the early morning temperature hovering around five degrees Celsius, the car's engine was still cold, not ready to be put through its paces. The engine spluttered and vibrated edgily in its compartment. But by the time I reached the city boundaries, heading south, it was purring and I was raring to go.

When the last of the city's stop-lights turned green, it threw open the road before me. I sped up and found myself rushing toward immense beauty: the black, purple, pink and orange of dawn in the Rhine valley, near its origins in the Alps. There was the instant thrill of being pressed into my seat, feeling the engine coming, then coming again, and again, as I shifted through the gears. It was a sensation of total immersion and bursting free, both at the same time.

Yet, the real thrill hadn't come from red-lining the engine in each gear and racing at top speed as it would have been with Kermit, but from the surging waves of acceleration. I suppose this isn't a thrill that Kermit could have ever given me, because acceleration – in the sense of power and thrust – is simply not something that the poor thing was capable of. In this rental of mine on that day, it was a different matter entirely. There was power and there was thrust and it made me realise that there is something out-of-this-world about accelerating in a car, as if we ourselves had superhuman strength, able to raise the world, like Atlas, effortlessly above our heads.

Raw speed, on the other hand, specially on public roads, had begun to give me flashes of fright and made me break out in sweat. With Kermit that was never a problem, really. That's because 141.5kmh, achieved only under perfect conditions – downhill, homesick and with the fan turned off – never felt all that threatening. But, 200kmh, achieved in less than thirty seconds, well, that, I noticed, gave me sweaty palms and heart palpitations. I recall that admitting to this really pained me because speed was, oh, so manly. What's more, didn't feeling fright mean another pleasure lost? That was rather disconcerting because it wasn't the only pleasure I had lost in recent times. For example, when I was younger I could enjoy the pleasure of the wind tousling my hair in an open-top car. Now, where once there had been a lush growth of hair, there was only a warped plane with sparse vegetation, and the best the wind could do was curl two strands of hair into a knot. So, yes, the possibility of losing yet another pleasure was a real concern at that time. But the more I thought about it, the more I realised that it wasn't so much a loss as an exchange. To my astonishment, I had discovered something else, namely that there was also a pleasure in knowing when to stop. It almost felt as if rushing along at high and higher speed had become not an affirmation of life, but a form of death. And so I was happy on that day to ease off and relax the bounding and leaping forward into cruising at comfortable speed.

About an hour later, the sun rose and divided the world in two, the still-dark valleys below and the glorious mountains above. In fact, I had finished climbing my first mountain, the Bielerhöhe, which separates Austria's two western-most states, and was already descending into a Tyrolean valley, negotiating hairpin turns on the way down, one after another.

The only way I can describe driving among those mountains on that day is as a sensation of near-flight. Gliding along those perfect mountain roads let me soar and sink,

"I found myself
rushing toward
immense beauty: the black, purple, pink
and orange of dawn…"

"About an hour later, the sun rose and divided the world into two, the still-dark valleys below and the glorious mountains above."

climb and descend, and in these motions partake in the sensations unique to flight, at once accelerating forward, upward and sideways. On those mountain roads, I could almost become a bird, almost sense the thrills as paragliders do. Instead of thermals, it was the engine's power that propelled me to gain height. The road, rather than limiting my freedom, shaped my mood by setting my course, as the wind shapes the paraglider's flight. At times, I slowly glided higher along a straight path. At others, I spiralled upward along serpentine twists and, atop a saddle, came to a standstill, floating in mid-air. Then I fell and compressed in the approach of a sharp hairpin turn, only to take off again in swooping arches of rising elevation. That morning, I frolicked, I played, as I had done many times before, for hours and hours, diving into broad valleys and shooting up across sharp peaks, forgetting about the world left underneath. The engine's power and sounds and my adrenaline combined to keep me going, and going, with a complete loss of the sense of time. Had I been at it for a few minutes? For an hour? For two or three? I couldn't remember. I do know what I wasn't thinking: where is my stopwatch? By sharp contrast, when I had been on these roads with Kermit many years ago I would not have been caught dead without a stopwatch. Why? Because what was the point of climbing a mountain, other than to do it in the shortest possible time? Yet, on that autumn day, the thought of a stopwatch, the thought of any measure of time, could not have been further from my mind.

After the descent from the mountains surrounding the Bielerhöhe, the valley opened up and the road wound along the frothy, blue-green river Trisanna in Tyrol. The turns were no longer sharp and twisty, but broad and lush. Some bends were drawn as if with a circle. Others started off tight, only to open up wide onto the next straight. Yet others were more deceptive, all inviting and sweeping at first, but then curling up snugly. Accompanied by my favourite on-the-road music, how enjoyable it was to dance along this road.

Sitting on the roadside bench after my morning drive, I wondered why it was that I enjoyed driving to music so much. In the Kermit days, it had all been rather simple. Even in the midst of winter when driving through a village on a busy day, I would crank up the heat so that I could comfortably roll down the windows without freezing, all in order to make sure that my favourite music, blaring out of my hamlet-blaster speakers would be heard by as many passers-by as possible. That's it. It was that simple.

On that drive I was thinking something entirely different, however. From the tapping of two fingers to the pounding of the heart, from the writhing of the body to the shedding of a tear, music had always created and amplified my moods. There is music that puts me to sleep. There is music that makes me angry. There is music that makes me march. And then there is music that makes me dance. How does it do that, I wondered? Could it be that music made me feel like dancing because it made my body resonate to its tune, just like the body of a violin resonates to its string, turning a quiet sound into one that is loud and proud? Could it be that the amplification had been greater still because I resonated with my car, together as one, to the emotions created by my favourite music? Perhaps, but…oh, so intellectual! And in need of simplification: rarely does the pendulum swing from one extreme in one single sweep straight to its resting position.

These bends along the river Trisanna had not only been the perfect place to let music move me, they were also a delight to practise finding the ideal line, that invisible ribbon on a road that marks the quickest way through a turn. The ideal line. Now that really brought back memories of racetracks, pitch-black rubber on dark-grey tarmac, screeching sounds, bodies – my body! – filled to the brim with testosterone and similar juices in the pursuit of speed and the perfection that lay in shaving off ten, five, nay, even one hundredth of a second. All that could not have been further from the pleasure I experienced on that day. So what was it? What was it if not speed? I recall giving it a lot of thought, but I don't think I managed to figure it out. That didn't come until a lot later when one day I saw a collie facing in the driving direction and sitting on the flat bed of a pick-up truck that was cruising along a winding road. As I was driving behind this truck, I was fascinated by the leaning into each bend of that pooch, its long mane fluttering in the wind, as she yelped with excitement. She was apparently having immense fun. Right then it hit me: the fun of going through turns didn't come so much from the thrill of speed as it came from the challenge of balancing. What's more, it's a fun that has evidently come down to us from times immemorial. After all, this pup had fun, and she was of a species just a tad older than ours. (Although

"Accompanied by my favourite music,
how **enjoyable** it was
to dance along this road..."

sometimes one wonders.) And sure enough, once it hit me, I could see the fun in balancing everywhere, from leaning into a strong wind to balancing a bicycle at rest.

That's also precisely where my enjoyment came from on that day along the beautiful bends of the river Trisanna. After all, what was the pleasure of driving on the ideal line if not the pleasure of balancing my car, turn after turn after turn? On top of that, there was the desire to experience perfection. I recall feeling a big let-down when I sensed that I was way off the ideal line through a sequence of turns. In fact, the urge was so strong that I was often tempted to turn around, to have another go at zipping through a turn, just because I had messed it up on the first try. In the end I never did, probably for reasons that lie deeply buried in my psyche and are better left unexplored.

In Landeck – a quaint town presided over by a beautiful medieval castle, visible from the road – the Trisanna runs into the river Inn. I followed the Inn for a little while and then turned right toward Ötz, that is south toward Italy. From there it was a drive forward in time, from the last vestiges of summer through the leaflessness of autumn and, as I climbed the winding road toward the 2,474 meter high Timmelsjoch, right into winter. Only a few days earlier, a bad weather front had crossed the Alps. It had left the valleys drenched and the mountaintops dusted with snow. While I had secretly hoped that some of the snow remained – my passion for driving on snow being undiminished – I suspected that the still-warm autumn rays had already melted it all away. As I gained altitude, I began to notice lumps of snow on the pastures and fields of rocks lining the road. By the time I reached Hochgurgl (2,154m), everything was covered in snow, except for the road, which had been meticulously cleared. I continued to climb, perhaps another hundred meters in elevation. Then, for the first time, there were spots of snow on the road where evidently the sun did not reach at this time of year, even at midday. Up a few more turns, and the spots grew into patches, reaching further into the centre of straight sections of road. The turns themselves still held out, being wet, not snowy. Another bend or two and, at last, the road was completely covered with snow and sparsely sprayed with loose grit to improve traction. Now steady. First, get a feel for the grip of the rental on this snow-covered surface. Step on the brake hard, and see what's on offer. Ah, that's good, there is still quite a bit of traction. This snow was perfect. Not slithery and slimy, but cold, pressed and crystalline. Turning in was also no problem. In the next turn, it was time to try out what I'd been thirsting for. At the apex of this hairpin turn, where I'd be in first gear on dry tarmac, I deliberately stayed in second so as not to have too much power on my rear wheels. Then I gave the accelerator a brief shove and, sure enough, the rear end broke out. I reduced the power, but kept the throttle open, leaning my body into, yet steering against the turn's direction. *Et voila!* I was drifting at a slight angle through the turn. As the turn opened up, I relaxed my counter-steer, the car began to straighten out, and I saw a gendarme ogling me with wide-open eyes. What on earth was he doing at this god-forsaken place, and at this time of day? For a split-second I thought it would be safe to

ignore him for he surely didn't trust what his eyes were seeing, but that was as unlikely as a cuckold not trusting his eyes when finding his wife in bed with another man. Sure enough, he signalled me to pull over. While I slowed down, I contrasted how I might have dealt with this situation in my youth, and how my more mature self would react. The difference could not have been starker. Should I admit that I had lost it – that my car sliding at a good angle was all an accident of miserable driving – in order to give me a fighting chance of avoiding a fine? Or would I admit no such thing, instead proudly proclaiming: "You're darn right. I just made my car do this. I love sliding on snow. So there!"? When I was young, that's exactly what I would have said. I would also have had to pay an outrageous fine. But I would never, ever have admitted that I had lost it. On that day, however, I wasn't so sure. Actually, not true; it was never really a question. I admitted without hesitation or shame to being a bungling idiot – and got off with nothing but a warning.

As soon as I was on the road again, I trod easy until the point where the gendarme couldn't see me any longer. Then I was tempted to go at it again, but not having Kermit's key accessories with me – friend, shuffle, bag of snow chains – I decided to temper my desire.

Instead, I soaked up the sensation of driving on snow, of biting into snow, almost as if to taste it. It was a sensation I had never really felt before. I suppose, whenever I hit snow in Kermit, I was so busy balancing the car at the acutest angle possible that there was no time for tasting, for savouring anything at all; there was only time for hanging on. But here I was, shunning the thrill of a ninety-degree angle and, instead, tasting the flavour of snow. No, I didn't get out and eat it. I just felt it through the steering wheel; I savoured it and soaked it up through how it made my rental wriggle and quiver. I loved it. And it made me think. I had always loved the sensation of driving on different shapes of roads – going straight, along winding roads and up and down mountains – but, hey, that didn't really compare to tasting the unique surfaces of roads – hot or wet tarmac, loose gravel or slippery snow. If I only ever knew the pleasures of shapes, but not that of surfaces of roads, it would almost be as if all I could do was touch food, but never taste it. The real pleasure, it dawned on me that day, came from zooming right in to where the food hits the palette or the rubber hits the road. By way of example, did you know that adding salt to certain ingredients – tomatoes, say – makes them taste sweeter, not saltier? It's this kind of detail that I'm talking about.

Let me take you back with me to a driving experience in the U.S., some years later, an experience that really packed it in when it came to tasting the distinct flavours of roads.

It was a scorching summer day. I was driving from Gallup, New Mexico, on the I-40 toward Flagstaff in Arizona, right between the Petrified Forest National Park and the Painted Desert. It must have been around 40 degrees Celsius. The relentless sun had brought the pitch black tarmac to a simmer hours earlier and from there to a bubbling boil. The air shimmered and placed hallucinations of puddles of water between the horizon and me.

The road felt, above all, reliable, even familiar, because it was firm and offered a lot of grip. But because of the heat the ribbed and fried-to-a-light-crisp tarmac also tasted mellow and tender, like a fine cut of beef, grilled to perfection. And the sizzling sound of the tyres positively added to the sensation.

Now, there is something beautifully reassuring about biting into a piece of tenderloin, and it was just as reassuring to drive on that hot tarmac. At times, it lulled me into a state of stupor and drew me into aimless thought, munching on the road absent-mindedly in my elephantine four-wheel drive. At others, the tarmac's clinginess prompted me to eat up the road on the straights and make the tyres sing, softly, throughout many turns. That hot, boiling asphalt was a surface like no other.

Later that day, after an all-American lunch (BLT, hold the mayo; fully transparent coffee with artificial sweetener) served by an all-American waitress ("Hi, I am Patsy, and I'll be your waitress today!") at an all-American diner ("We trust in God. All others pay cash!"), I had planned to leave Flagstaff on route 180 toward the Grand Canyon. I was looking forward to a bit of diversion. The I-40 was mostly straight. Route 180, on the other hand, had bends, quite a few of them, at least from Flagstaff to Valle where it began heading due north.

By the time I hit the road, it was about four in the afternoon and the morning's dry heat

"Hi, I am **Patsy** and I'll be your waitress today!"

had transformed into sweltering humidity. Thick clouds, not bright white but ominously grey, had grouped together in a huddle and threatened a shower. For a while the rain had held off, but then, with a bolt of lightening, it came with a vengeance. About thirty miles into route 180, the sky opened as I had never seen it before. This wasn't rain. It was as if a dam had broken in the heavens above, swamping all underneath. Now, I am no pussy when it comes to driving in the rain, but just this once I was tempted to pull over and sit it out. And so I did. The assault lasted for only 20 minutes, whereupon deluge changed into fine drizzle.

Then I got back on the road, opened the window a bit and enjoyed little gusts of wind and water droplets tickle my skin. They wiped away the stupor of the morning completely and left me totally refreshed and perceptive to the world. That was a good thing because driving on that soaked tarmac was a very different kind of experience.

At first, these hosed-down roads felt as firm and gripping as the dry ones of the morning. But that was a deception that didn't last long, for every now and then I found myself, without warning, on a patch of standing water. Instantly, that reassuring grip gave way to the slipperiness of hydroplaning, a sudden sting that stiffened my back and sent a surge of adrenaline through my veins. It reminded me of letting my teeth sink into a tuna sushi where, between fresh raw meat and rice there hides a bit too much wasabi. At first, that ribbed, red tuna gives the appearance of the firmness and tastiness of a tender steak. Bite into it, however, and it all feels softer, squishier. And then the sting, this time from too much of that zealous radish, that makes the experience as memorable as the many sudden slips that I experienced that afternoon in my less-than-perfectly balanced four-wheel drive.

As I kept going, however, the nervousness and prickliness gave way to a sense of feeling totally alive. The hissing of my elephant's tyres, the glossiness of the road, trees and rocks, the dense vapour spewed out by the occasional car ahead of me, sensitised my mind and made my muscles nimble. Never had I felt so strongly the pleasures of driving in the rain.

In fact, I felt so boyish then, that the puddles on the road exerted an unfailing attraction: I just wanted to make them splash, the harder the better. With the wipers going at top

"The air shimmered and placed

hallucinations

of puddles of water between the horizon and me..."

"For a while the rain held off,

but with one bolt of lightning,

it came with a vengeance."

speed, I aimed at big roadside puddles to catch them halfway between their side and centre. Each time, this sent a big arc of water splashing out from underneath my elephant's wheels, which, if I had gotten it just right, would come crashing back down on it, as though spraying its back with its trunk. On the empty route 180 that afternoon, it felt as good as taking a refreshing outdoor shower myself. And then, a little later, when the rain had stopped and the sun reappeared, pungent-sweet steam rose from the cool tarmac, tantalising my nostrils and tickling my eyes.

The following day I spent at the Grand Canyon, doing what tourists do: walking along the rim, donkey-riding into the Canyon, gathering statistics. Most memorably, I took a helicopter ride to the sound of the opening movement of Richard Strauss's Thus Spake Zarathustra as the chopper approached the rim and then, to even greater effect, sank abruptly into the gorge. It was a stimulating experience. It also left me wanting to get back on the road early the next day.

I was heading west and wanted to take portions of the classic route 66 from Williams to Kingman. But instead of getting there directly on paved roads, I had a craving for a bit of off-road adventure. So, I let my hotel know where I was going (just in case), packed a silly amount of water and food (donuts – also just in case) and set off.

Now, when I say off-road adventure, I don't really mean what true men mean when they clear their throats to tell you a story. No, I am afraid, I wasn't then (nor am I now) into monster trucks or near-death experiences. Also, discussions about vehicle clearances needed to cross forbidding obstacles have always left me cold. I'm perfectly happy to drive around any obstacle, even small ones.

What I relished that day was something entirely different. It was, first, throwing giant clouds of dust into the air. Seeing everything covered with sand, pebbles and rocks, hearing the rumble and tumble, the knocking and cracking of bits and pieces flying everywhere, gave me a beautiful sense of driver-seat adventure. Never mind that all I tasted was grit when I gnawed my teeth.

And then there was the taste of biting into something very special. Arizona's dirt roads were shaky, crumbly and flaky, but uniformly soft-textured with a firm underside. What did they remind me of? Donuts, anyone? Or was it altogether different, more like walking barefoot on small marbles? The base and the marbles are hard, yet the overall sensation is not firm at all. The surface feels loose, moving and soft.

How different this was from dry or wet tarmac. Of course, there was far less grip than on asphalt. But it also didn't give way as abruptly as when I had hit puddles hiding in grooved tracks a couple of days before. The loss of grip neither sneaked up on me nor whacked me over the head. Instead, grip slowly gave way, changed in degree, not kind. So, I felt ready to push myself the instant I hit the gravel road.

Even after several hours of sliding, swerving and skidding along the back roads of Arizona, accompanied to the beating rhythms of my very own off-road Buddha Bar compila-

"What a let-down it was:
it was **sealed**
all the way."

tion ("Another one bites the dust"), I recall that I just couldn't wipe the grin off my face. Driving on that loose gravel at a decent clip, with the bonnet of my elephant gently swaying from one side to the other, left me totally engrossed. I loved the balancing act of keeping the elephant moving straight with easy tugs at the wheel and tapping my left foot on the floor board as I ploughed through the rugged, cacti-decorated wilderness of Arizona. When eventually I saw the intersection with Route 66 up ahead, I was downright disappointed. Route 66 is a stunning road, but, heavens, what a let-down it was, if for no other reason than this: it was sealed all the way.

So yes, attuning my senses to the delicious surfaces of roads – soaking wet, sizzling hot, bouncy gravely or slippery snowy – has ever since meant a special pleasure. At any rate, hitting a bit of left-over snow near the Timmelsjoch pass on that Autumn Sunday morning wasn't the end of that day's drive. As luck had it, once over the top of that pass, the road was dry, not snow-covered, since the air on the South side of the Alps was, as is often the case, a few degrees warmer than in the North. And so, approaching each turn as I descended into the valley, I continued to feel exhilaration in slowing and shifting down with heel-and-toe.

Toward the end of the descent and just before entering St. Leonhard, there was a red light controlling traffic going past road works. As I approached the light, I found myself taking pleasure in slowing down gingerly and then coming to rest softly. Now that, I recall saying to myself, provided incontrovertible evidence, if by then any more was needed, that the days of my youth were irretrievably lost. In the past, "slowing down" was a missing entry in the dictionary and "coming to rest" was what I did in a hammock. If I really did need to stop, it was with a screech. But no longer. On that day, I realised that over the years I had begun to enjoy slowing down and coming to rest in a very different way. What's more, the enjoyment was as intense as the excitement of screeching to an abrupt halt used to be. I suppose, it was another one of those cases, "My youth is dead! Long live being young!"

And wherein exactly lay this new-found enjoyment? It was in coming to rest without the slightest jolt, in making the transition from motion to non-motion, in leaping across this infinity with the softest touch. It was about coming to rest so smoothly that a blindfolded passenger could not tell whether the car was still in motion or not. I had come to relish these

"...hearing the rumble and tumble, the knocking and cracking of bits and pieces flying everywhere gave me a beautiful sense of driver-seat adventure..."

moments so much that it now pains me to see others (or, heavens, catch myself in a momentary lapse into sanity) stepping on the brake uniformly until the car stops with a jerk, rocking back and forth to regain its balance. How clumsy! There is an art in coming to rest, which requires reducing the pressure on the brake in direct proportion to the slowing down of the car so that I stop braking at the precise moment, no, a split-second before, the car comes to a full stop. Then, there is no rocking, no jerking, only silky cat paws, standing still.

Before long, the red light turned green, and I drove off in search of my sandwich lunch.

Soon afterwards, I arrived at my resting place, where I was leaning back on the wooden bench, still soaking up the warm autumn sun. On that day, I realised that more had changed than I had ever noticed before. Old pleasures had given way to new. What an unforgettable day it had been on those stunning, absolutely perfect roads. Excuse me? What did I just say: perfect roads? Oh my! *Plus ça change, plus c'est la même chose!* While that day had conclusively proven to me that my driving enjoyment was no longer tied up with owning a Ten for a car, could it be that it had come to depend on finding perfection elsewhere? To be precise, on driving on perfect roads – deliciously winding, covered with yummy surfaces, and free of other cars? If so, how much progress had I actually made? Some, I suppose, because the desire to own a perfect car speaks of a sort of despicable preoccupation with ostentatious possessions, whereas seeking enjoyment on roads is a more acceptable form of consumption – after all, roads, even perfect ones, are public goods, there for all to enjoy. But the chase after the perfect this-that-or-the-other obviously continued to run red-hot, and so, something was clearly still missing.

And yet, on this black ribbon, lives are made **free and dreams** are played out.

Being on the road,when
moments
are born.

All turning motions
cast on us a spell
Be it **skiing** on white powder
Be it **skating** on blue ice
Be it **surfing** on black waves
Or be it **driving,** turn after turn,
into fleeting dusk.

CHAPTER FOUR

Fulfilment

"The moon belongs to everyone; the best things in life are free." – *Buddy De Sylva.*

Quite a few years have passed since that memorable drive. And, with the passage of time, two further things changed. For one, I gave up my dream of owning a perfect car and replaced it with a workhorse, a Bordeaux-coloured Porsche 911. You might say, well, well, well, that's not exactly an average car either. True, but it's a lot further away from super-car status than it is close to cars made by Audi or Vauxhall. (For example, it's slower than quite a few Audis and barely has the visual allure of some Vauxhalls.)

I've had it for some years now and will probably keep it for several more. I like it because it is so perfectly imperfect, despite being German. It has all the right things for me, and none that gets in my way. It's got four-wheel drive and I was able to buy snow tyres for use in winter without being given a look that said "You've got to be joking!" It starts every time, no matter how cold. It's got reasonable ground clearance so I can drive down and up underground car parks where I let it sleep without hesitation. It does just enough for my ego, but without enhancing it to the point where even I can't stand myself. It's not particularly good looking, but no ugly duckling either. It doesn't have any of the modern stability-enhancing electronics (except for ABS); therefore, I know what it does; and I don't have to second-guess its second-guessing me. It's so practical a car that if I were inclined to go on a holiday with a caravan trailer, who knows, I might even hitch it with my 911. Nah, I'd be too embarrassed for that.

It really is the perfect contrast to my perfect car. Whereas my perfect car was a capricious lady that had taken my reason away, the 911 is an intelligent woman, which, as Paul Valéry has astutely observed, is a women with whom one can be as stupid as one wants. And for all these reasons, it's a great, if by no means cheap, everyday car.

As a consequence, my relationship with it is healthy and balanced. I haven't given it a name; nor have I dressed it up with make-up or tuning kits. It's got lots of chipped paint and its face is a graveyard of instantly dead bugs. It's got no extras that didn't come with it when I bought it and it would probably choke on a dose of air-freshener as I once did when I inhaled, by accident, a draw of my first cigar. In other words, it hasn't been spoiled and I, when one day I sell it, will probably not shed a tear.

* * *

The other thing that's changed – hard though it is to believe – is this: whether or not I enjoy myself driving these days depends a lot less on where I am driving or what's happening around me. Instead, I've discovered that finding pleasure in driving is a matter of outlook, almost as easily had on the way to work as on ever more winding, ever more perfect roads or in ever more spectacular landscapes.

Hearing me say this, you could be forgiven for thinking that, in all likelihood, I have spent three months in a Buddhist retreat in Northern Thailand to cleanse my soul, or that I have had, finally, a near-death experience somewhere beyond 250kmh. Sorry, nothing nearly as juicy as that. Instead, I made a memorable encounter on a work-related trip, early on a humdrum Friday morning in Germany, a place not usually known for bumping into elusive spiritual enlightenment. I left Düsseldorf in my 911 at 8:15 in the morning for a meeting in Brussels at 11am. Since I would easily cover the 250+ kilometre trip in the time available, I was in no big hurry.

Traffic was reasonably dense on the A44 at this time in the morning but the fog had begun to lift and had revealed a pale, blue sky. I was in a good, relaxed mood, a mood that these days always makes me pull back from the passing left into the regular right lane so as to make room for others, even when there is no one in sight. It normally bugs me when folks stay in the passing lane well after the reason for being there – a car to be passed – has disappeared. When I asked a German friend why it is that Germany's passing lanes are always stuffed silly, more than those of any other country, he informed me that there are three, precisely three, types of drivers in his country. First, there are those who genuinely drive fast. Second, there are those who fear never being able to get back into the passing lane if ever they left it. And, third, there are those who drive precisely at 130kmh (Germany's "Richtgeschwindigkeit", loosely translated as the "politically correct speed") and stay put in the passing lane because they want to lecture everyone else about what is proper behaviour. That's why on occasion I deliberately pull back from the passing lane, even when there is no good reason for me to leave it since I, like, really, need to be passing another car in just a second. Why do I pull back? Because, well, I feel tempted to counter-lecture. I must admit that this is a childish, even contemptible, yet worse, schoolmasterly, act of doing onto others precisely as I would not have them do onto me. But it must be done, on occasion. Yet, on this day I was genuinely in the mood to give way and to be neighbourly.

So, it was with a bit of irony that my attention fell on a Smart driving several cars ahead of me. I don't recall exactly where it was, but reasonably close to Aachen, a large town on the way to Brussels. This Smart was going at full speed, which, in the case of a Smart, amounted to 135kmh. (It's amazing how these days a car that does 135kmh is called Smart;

"Square boxes on wheels
are not supposed to be doing this."

twenty-five years ago a car that was doing 135kmh was called Renault.) I noticed him not for the unremarkable 135kmh, but because he too was moving in and out of the passing lane and, more curiously, because he did so with incomparable swiftness. With the full thrust of his 135kmh he closed in on trucks or buses, which were moving slower than he in the regular lane. When he was about to crash into them (well, that's what it looked like from far behind), he switched out into the passing lane, in a zigzag motion, without missing a beat. No sooner was he in the passing lane than he zoomed by the slower car. Once past, he jumped back into the right-hand lane, zigzag, seemingly only with inches to spare. All the while he kept to his constant 135kmh, his brake lights not coming on even once.

I was fascinated for I had never seen a car, a real car, albeit a small one, jump lanes like this. Square boxes on wheels are not supposed to be doing this. It looked as out-of-place as when a Smart is parked at a 90-degree angle in a row of street-aligned cars. It's just not meant to be, but here it was, right under my nose.

The driver was, clearly, enormously skilled. And it wasn't his first day of doing this either. He judged precisely his own car's speed versus that of others. Not only did he judge the relative speeds spectacularly well, he also had an innate sense of distances and motion. As far as I could tell, he never cut anybody off, although he did manage to give some a bit of a fright with his skilful and considerate, but swift and abrupt manoeuvres.

Each time it went like this: two quick motions of his wrist, first left, then back to straight again; that put him into the passing lane. Three-four seconds later, two reflex-like motions again, right, then back to straight, and here he was in the regular lane once more. In and out. In and out. Whoosh! Whoosh! Whoosh! A sight to behold. A slapstick movie in fast-forward.

As I approached him (he was in the regular, I in the passing lane), he eyed me in his rear view mirror as he himself was approaching a truck. What to do? I could sense him calculate, nay, feel with his eyes and his motion bone the speeds of the three parties: truck (in front), 911 (me behind) and Smart (himself in between). And I did the same: I judged the speeds and distances. What to do? His verdict was to stay put in his lane. He sensed that his distance to the truck was large enough to let me pass, allowing him time to jump out into the passing lane, between me and the next car.

My verdict was different. I wanted to give him space so he could pass the truck. Not only that, I also wanted to hold on to my front-and-centre seat for yet another performance of this flee-jump artist. My contrary verdict, my desire to watch him perform, caught him off guard. He hadn't considered (let alone counted on) my slowing down. But he noticed it in an instant. As soon as my giving way had sunk in, he smiled – I could see it in his rear view mirror – and put out his right-hand turn signal: blink once, blink twice. For a split second I thought, "Ah, he's getting out at the next exit." But no, that wasn't it. He'd signalled that he'd prefer it if I passed him. So, I sped up again, under the spell of a magician who was clearly planning each of his acts with delicious attention to detail.

Once I was even with him, I saw him wave at me. I waved back. He also continued to wear a broad, animated smile that mixed a bit of gratitude with a big dose of surprise, for he could tell that he, in his Smart, had drawn the attention and admiration of someone in a much more powerful car. I sensed that this was a rare occasion for him. More often his precision and thoughtful driving – he made perfect use of the passing lane, using it only for what it was intended and only as briefly as was humanly possible – would be frowned upon and dismissed as silly shenanigans. Yet nothing could have been further from the truth. He knew it, and he was pleased that someone else knew it as well.

But his smile said something else. Here was a man who was in perfect control of his car. He revelled in the skill it took to do what he was doing. Plus he was clearly enjoying his day-to-day commute. Ennui most certainly wasn't a problem for him. No, the daily commute was an opportunity to have fun, 10, 20, maybe 50 times on his way to work, at least as many times on the way home again. There was excitement and fun and, occasionally, admiration to be found each time when he - whoosh! - jumped out to pass, and - whoosh! - jumped back in to complete a practised manoeuvre.

Just as soon as I was past him, he was at it again: within a split second, he was right behind me, with no more than a few inches between my and his bumper. That lasted for all but a second, for then I was gone. But in my rear view mirror, I saw him continue to practise his art, dance to his tune, at a constant 135kmh, the headlights not dipping once. Some people know how to live, how to make much out of little, where others make little of much. And if in the future I read about a Smart doing summersaults, I will chuckle, because far from being disbelieving, I will know it must be him!

* * *

In a way, the discovery that enjoying my life meant learning how to make much of little marked the end of the journey toward my boundless enjoyment of the pleasures of driving. But in another way, it wasn't the end. Instead, it was a new beginning: I still had to learn how to get along with others. And so the journey continued.

How can it be that many make so **little** of much, when she, right now, makes so **much** of little?

CHAPTER FIVE

Camaraderie

"One of the most common defects of half-instructed minds is to think much of that in which they differ from others, and little of that in which they agree with others."
– Walter Bagehot.

During the days that I was flooring my Kermit, all drivers fell neatly into two main categories: either obstacles to be removed or challenges to be overcome. These days, the world's drivers still fall into two main categories, but the categories are slightly different: those driving faster than I (the ugly), and those driving slower (the bad). The former are clearly crazy; the latter obviously idiotic. And then there are the good, the few, like that life-affirming Smart driver described in the previous chapter, with whom I really hit it off.

Actually, this represents a monumental shift in how I relate to other people. For one, my nemeses are no longer categorised in absolute, but instead in more relative terms – crazy or idiotic. These may not be the most endearing of appellations, but note: at least they do allow for shades of grey. For another, there are also people I can get on with. They may be few and far between, but they do exist. Now that's progress.

To illustrate my point, I vividly recall one day that really packed it in: two goods, one bad, one ugly, and quite a few others besides.

It all started with a phone call from an acquaintance who, to spare you the details, had made good and was now living in Barcelona. During the conversation, he let it drop that he had treated himself and bought an Aston Martin.

"Come on down some time, and I'll let you drive it," he suggested.

"Yeah, right, that'll be the day," I thought to myself. I do get these offers on occasion, but in most cases, nothing ever happens. Despite my having kicked the habit of lusting after the perfect car, I find this cruel, like dangling a bone with juicy marrow in front of a drooling dog with the words "Only testing." So, I stopped drooling and forgot about this offer right after I hung up.

As it happened, however, I did find myself in Barcelona about six months later. Two days before I was due to arrive, I gave my Aston Martin owning acquaintance a call, not expecting much. To my surprise, not only did he not put the phone down as soon as he heard me speak, he actually said, "Why don't you stay with us for the night?!" And then added: "You must drive my Aston Martin."

I was perplexed. This was not supposed to happen. But it didn't take long for my surprise to give way to boundless anticipation. I was really going to drive an Aston Martin. This was going to be a special day: elegance; superiority; British Racing green; Connolly leather in tastefully matching beige. What else could it be?

When I arrived at my friend's house – in my worldview he was now no longer a mere acquaintance, but a very close, Aston Martin owning, friend – I immediately spotted his car, and nearly fainted. It was in Rothesay red! A garish red, with an ivory – almost white – interior! I stood there for a while, frozen solid and immovable like a stalagmite, and let the disappointment sink in. It looked like a strawberry cheesecake: heavy on the strawberry, light on the white cream. While I could get used to the red, I suppose, I couldn't get over the near-white interior. I could never have a light interior like this because my 911 doubles up as my mobile home. That means, for example, that I eat in it. Little bits of fries, the remnants of a Happy Meal, in among the stitching of the leather, well, that's manageable if not pretty, but blotches of ketchup on this kind of ivory-coloured upholstery would surely be the wrong kind of colour-coordination.

After I had composed myself, I rang the doorbell.

My acquaintance – he had already dropped back down in status since my friendship can be bought, but there is a limit – opened the door with the words, "Isn't it beautiful!"

"Oh, yes… very… imaginative," was all that I could muster.

By the time we had finished with dinner, I had come back to my senses. The objective was to experience driving a great car, not to win a beauty contest. So, I asked my acquaintance what he had had in mind when he offered to let me drive his Aston.

"Well, have it; it's yours for the day tomorrow," he replied.

I couldn't believe it. An Aston Martin for a whole day in Spain! What a good friend my acquaintance really was. "In that case, do you mind if I drive up to Andorra and back? It's a place I've never been to."

He nodded and smiled.

Before going to bed, I studied the map and decided that I would drive up to Andorra, from there to Toulouse, and then back via Perpignan to Barcelona. A full programme, but doable. I fell asleep quickly and dreamed gibberish dreams about cheesecake and twelve cylinders.

I woke up at 7:30. The previous day's blue sky and sunshine had given way to dense cloud. Since my mood rises and falls with the weather, this was not good news. But never mind, in just a few minutes I would be driving an Aston Martin. So, I jumped out of bed and was ready to go within fifteen minutes. It was going to be a beautiful day nonetheless, filled with leisurely, gentlemanly, but spirited driving. As it should be in an Aston.

My friend appeared from his bedroom, apparently woken by my stirrings. He looked rather sleepy at 7:45am on this Saturday morning, so I politely declined his offer to give me detailed directions.

"Thank you very much, but you go back to bed. I'll be alright. Look, I have detailed maps and a good sense of direction. What's more, all roads lead to Andorra, don't they? I'll be back tonight. Thank you so very much!" With that I set off.

About twenty minutes later I was lost in labyrinthine Barcelona. Well, not lost exactly, no self-respecting man ever is; I just didn't know where I was going.

Coming on top of the morose weather, this was not a promising start. But it would all be well just as soon as I found my way onto the A81, the highway leading toward Andorra.

I had almost been on the A81 a few minutes earlier when I had made it onto a feeder to this highway, but had missed the exit to the highway itself. So, I took the next exit – why is it that "the next exit" is always so far away? – in order to find my way back to the feeder. Fortunately, there were very few cars on this Saturday morning, so I dared to read the Barcelona city map on my lap while I continued to drive. After a few turns, I caught a glimpse of the long, right-turning ramp that would take me to the feeder. I manoeuvred in its direction and made it onto the ramp alright, then ambled up, still half-reading the map in order to avoid making the same mistake twice.

It was then that I simultaneously heard a high-pitch noise and saw a flash of light in my rear view mirror. My first thought was: "Oh no. The police! I must have done something wrong. Reading a map while driving? That's just what I need!" But no, it wasn't the police. I was relieved, but only for a second, since I was forced to make the acquaintance of a youngster on a monstrous motorbike, sitting only a few feet behind my rear bumper. My bright red Aston had apparently drawn his attention.

"Oh no! The **police!**"

The timing was poor. At that moment I was, as you know, directionally challenged. I was in a very expensive car that belonged to a friend with odd tastes. Who knew what he'd do if the darn thing was busted? I had barely driven five kilometres. Sure, I'd sorted out the gears, but not the car's handling. I was in the mood for relaxation, not racing. The sky was overcast. And I felt old, very old. So, I withdrew into my shell and decided to bide my time.

As is often the case, the lack of response produced the opposite result: he was all the more goaded by it. He raised his left hand and made swooping and lifting motions that left no doubt about what he wanted me to do. It wasn't what I wanted to do, so, I took a deep breath and carried on up the ramp at a steady pace.

As the ramp straightened out, I heard him shift down a gear. Just as soon as we were on the feeder, he pulled past me, slowly. He looked at me, shook his head and veered into my lane just in front of me. From there, he turned his head and, staring at me, once again made his "C'mon, go for it!" motions. When he still didn't get what he wanted, he shifted down once more, then bolted forward like the devil, pulling his bike up on its rear wheel where he kept it for at least 200 metres. And then he was gone. Good riddance to him, the ugly. Surely this was just a bad start to an otherwise fine day.

I was now on the A18 heading north and settled into a relaxed 130kmh, just a tiny bit above the 120kmh speed limit. I was in the passing lane, zooming by slower cars and buses and felt on top of the world, even – dare I say it – shoulders above the rest in the Aston Martin. The driving was effortless and relaxing, exactly the way I had imagined it.

Just when I had put the whole unpleasant episode behind me and had begun to daydream with excitement about driving across the Pyrenees later on that day, I was rudely brought back down to earth.

I was, as I said, in the passing lane. A hundred meters ahead, in the right-hand lane, I saw a slow-moving car following a tourist bus. My guess was they were doing 80kmh at best. In situations like this, I briefly flash my lights to alert the slower cars gently that a faster car is approaching. I deliberately avoid the horn because it can be mistaken as a sign of aggression. No, I flash my lights, just for an instant. In fact, if I could make my headlights smile, I would.

So, as much out of habit than anything else, I flashed my lights at the duo of bus and car. Oh my, was this the wrong thing to do! Just as soon as I flashed my lights, I could see the crawler's big beady eyes flare up in his rear view mirror. I knew right away that this was bad news. In an instant he decided what needed to be done. He flicked on his indicator and pulled out into the passing lane. Was it because now was the time to pass the bus behind which he'd been contentedly driving for quite some time? No. It was because he had decided that I had to be reined in.

Oh well, I have seen this type of behaviour many times, which means I am generally prepared for it. Since I was in no big hurry, I didn't mind so very much. I had already recovered from the ugly, the sun was peeping through breaks in the cloud cover, and I was

"In fact, if I could make my **headlights smile,** I would."

driving my Aston Martin.

Unfortunately, it didn't end with slowing me down. No, I was in for a lecture, replete with wagging finger: "You are breaking the law. You can't do that!" was what his finger was saying. If there'd been a way to make me stand in the corner, that's what he would have made me do. I tried the conciliatory route and put on a broad grin. But that didn't work either. He started talking to himself and looked meaner than ever. Presumably he misinterpreted my smile as a sneer. I must admit I was never a good actor. So, I gave up, and decided to hang back to watch the spectacle unfold from a distance.

It took him ages to pass that bus. Once he had, he began the procedure of pulling back into the right lane. He ceremoniously turned on his right blinker and looked for a long time into his rear view mirror to make one hundred per cent sure that he wouldn't be cutting off the bus. Cutting off the bus? God Almighty, how could he? By then he had dithered for so long that the bus would have been barely visible in his rear view mirror. Eventually he did veer to the right, ever so slowly. Once he was out of the way, I sped up and he, the bad, dropped quickly out of my view.

But not out of my mind. First the ugly, now this bad. It made me wonder: even though he and I are carbon-based life forms with 99.9999% of our DNA in common, at this moment what dominated my thinking wasn't the 99.9999%, but the 0.0001% which made him so very different from me. Why is it that it's always the 0.0001% that gets us, that starts our quarrels, and not the 99.9999% that would have us live in harmony all along? Why is it that the smaller the differences, the larger they loom? Who knows? But one thing is certain: it is a fundamental defect of the human race. Another thing that is certain is that

this defect is precisely why it is so wickedly hard to get on with other people. It means that we have to cut away first the frightening apparitions of large-looming, but in the end non-essential, differences before we can get to the things we have in common and which actually count. Getting on with people is therefore hard work. And, in this light, making a friend, a real friend, is an indescribable treasure.

The traffic got thinner as I got further away from Barcelona and approached the legendary Montserrat with its spectacular mountain range of stone spires. The beauty and uniqueness of the landscape made me calm down. The world was, after all, not all gloom and doom. As if to prove the point, just before Manresa, the day took a turn for the better and I was in for a most welcome surprise. At exit 13, where the on-ramp merges with the lanes of the main highway, I spotted another Aston in identical Rothesay red. At first I couldn't believe what I was seeing. Is it possible, I wondered, that two people have such excruciatingly bad taste?" This thought was quickly replaced with another: "What a wonderful coincidence! Two Astons!" Or was it a wonderful coincidence? I immediately recalled that morning's encounter with the ugly. While I was readier to do a bit of speedy driving than I had been in the morning – the AM already fitted me like a glove and I now definitely knew where I was going – I still wasn't in the mood for racing, not least because I had once been pulled over by Spanish highway police. That had ended up as a two-hour affair that cost me a pretty penny. No, I definitely wasn't in the mood for that. So, what kind of encounter was this going to be? Another one in which tiny differences would soon loom frighteningly large?

As I passed him, I saw him accelerate in a

spurt; evidently he had spotted me as well. However, instead of immediately pulling even with me, he hung back for a while. Then he locked into the same speed as I. Was that the calm before the storm? We drove for a while in the passing lane at a slightly higher cruising speed than before, him a good three hundred metres behind me.

After a couple of minutes or so, he moved back into the right-hand lane. In his spot appeared someone with high beams flashing and going at a speed substantially higher than ours. Now, when I see someone who wants to go faster than me I make room for them, always, because I know how frustrating it is to be slowed down, intentionally or obliviously, by someone who hoards the passing lane. So, I moved into the right-hand lane as well.

While I waited for the faster car to get past me, I slowly but surely ran up against a crawler in my lane, which meant I needed to slow down. Meanwhile, the other strawberry had merged back into the passing lane, still going at the speed that we were erstwhile doing together. Since I was now going slower, I figured, oh well, I'll let him pass. As he approached, I saw him briefly flash his lights, as I always do as well. I looked at him through my rear view mirror, and guess what I saw? Two bright eyes wrapped into a broad, confident smile. My heart jumped. He had not flashed his lights as a warning to keep me in my lane. No, it was an invitation for me to pull out in front of him again. I happily obliged and did so swiftly by shifting down and accelerating hard to minimise the need for him to slow down. (But also because it was a good reason to feel again the mighty V12's shove in my back.) In a flash, I was out in the passing lane. I also nodded "Thanks" to him, and thought to myself: "I like this guy!" Already, we were both going at 150kmh.

Thus introduced to each other, we wove in and out of traffic, as if connected by an umbilical cord. After a little while, when I had pulled into the right-hand lane once again after passing another bus, I saw him gathering momentum behind me. Before long, he pulled even with and looked over at me. He still had his broad smile and gave me a thumbs-up in acknowledgement of our shared tastes. Shared tastes? For a split-second I was tempted to signal that this car wasn't really mine, but then didn't because admitting that this car wasn't mine was worse for my ego than tolerating the shame I felt over its colour. So, I looked over approvingly, noting how he sat in his car, his arms slightly angled and hands resting easy on the steering wheel. There was none of that I-am-a-racer-look-how-cool, leaning back with arms stretched out straight. (How can anyone drive like that? It's like trying to pick up food with chopsticks held at their very end.) No, this fellow was perfectly at ease with himself and his car. I also noticed something else: his car wasn't just a strawberry; it too was a strawberry cheesecake, decked out in the same ivory leather as mine. What is the world coming to?

The road past Berga and along the Plago de la Baélls grew increasingly winding. On several occasions we passed slower cars in tandem. Since I was leading, I tried as best as I could to pass only when there was enough room for both of us to do so comfortably. On occasion when I judged the opening to be long enough, he disagreed and hung back, only to catch up with me again a little later.

This perfect, wordless interaction reminded me of the many times I had driven in convoys with friends when I was young. This was always something rather special because we communicated with one another in our own wordless language. It started with simple signals that were plainly visible from car to car and expanded from there to include others that were well-established automotive signals, but to which we had given new meanings. And there were new signals altogether: hugging the side of the road meant "Clear to pass"; moving to the centre "Don't try!" With each signal sent and understood, our friendship deepened and the bond among us tightened. It was an excitement similar to when we succeed in a no-look pass in a game of basketball. (Not that I really know this first hand. I'm too short for that game, so I took a friend's word for it.) And, if you permit me an even wider excursion, it reminds me, through the romantic lens of a man in mid-life crisis, of an eerie natural phenomenon. Through this lens, I see in the misty morning light a single goose taking flight. Within a wing beat, another twenty follow, breaking from the water almost as a group, honking lustily, their wings pumping. Before they clear the birches on the shore, they begin to spread apart and take their positions behind the leader, each slot offset to the back and side of the one in front. Their formation makes a ruler-straight sheering line or, even more wondrously, a perfect V. Driving in a convoy of trusted friends is perhaps a little less wondrous, but feels like no less magical an expression of belongingness.

The closer we got to Bellver de Cerdanya, on the other side of the Serra de Cadí, the denser the on-coming traffic got. The number of trucks going in our direction, largely uphill, swelled as well. Passing eighteen-wheelers on winding mountain roads is always a challenge; even more so, if you're driving in tandem. So, it was a pleasant surprise when more than one of the Spanish truckers signalled us when there was room to pass. Left blinker on: don't try. Right blinker on: free to pass. And, without fail, they waved to us

"Geez, don't I wish I was driving what you are driving right now!"

from their cabins on high as we overtook them. We waved back at them through our open sunroofs, which elicited a flash of their lights in acknowledgement and just a hint of "Geez, don't I wish I was driving what you are driving right now!" (I must admit, I like truckers. They drive for a living and know everything there is to know about interacting with others. Plus many of them have a passion for driving. How else could they do what they do for a living?)

In the dark of the five kilometre long Túnel de Cadí we became two ordinary cars again, just four white and four red lights moving along like all others. This was just as well because right after the tunnel, my companion turned right onto the E9 toward Puigcerdà, and I kept going straight toward Bellver. As he veered off, he flashed his lights twice and waved. I tapped my brakes twice and waved in return. As soon as he disappeared, I felt a sense of loss, the loss of someone I never knew, yet had come to know so well.

As I continued, I thought how nice it would be if cars were equipped to exchange their owners' details by merely pressing a button as I can now do with my mobile phone. Wouldn't it be nice if we could stay in touch? Meet up again? Drive again together? Wouldn't it be nice to be able to turn a passing acquaintance into the beginning of a friendship at the touch of a button? But then again: what would be the point? I have a hard enough time keeping up with the friends I already have. The path to loneliness is often paved with good intentions to stay in touch.

Where the C1411 merges with the N260 – just a few kilometres after the Túnel de Cadí – the pace of the previous several hours was rudely slowed down by densely packed traffic, and the cloud cover became dense to match. The road from Bellver de Cerdanya snakes along the el Segre, a small stream flanked by lush green bushes most of the way. To the left were spread out the hills of the Serra de Cadí, a mountain range whose slopes were covered in rich vegetation that reached up as far as I could see on that day, right up to where the imaginary peaks lay, beyond a cover of clouds. To the right, the view was very different. The mountains of the Reserva Nacional de Cerdanya rose sharply to form the taller and more barren southern border of Andorra. The road through this valley was drawn red and green on my map, which told me that on a beautiful day it would have been well worth it for its scenery alone. On that day, however, I was blessed neither with sunshine nor the satisfaction of swinging from turn to turn along this enticingly winding road. No, I was pretty much stuck in bumper-to-bumper traffic.

Before long I wound up in Andorra, and was instantly caught by surprise. Never in my life had I seen so many car dealerships and car accessories shops in one place. "What is it with the Andorrans?" I thought. "Are they car mad or what? Do 67,000 people really need so many wheels?"

Driving through Andorra, I let one car merge after another, including a black Peugeot 205CTI, that I dimly noticed because it looked pretty beat up. At any rate, I felt great because I had discovered that instant popularity could be mine for nothing more than a

"Driving in a convoy of trusted friends
is perhaps less wondrous, but feels like no less
magical an expression of
belongingness..."

smile and a willingness to let strangers merge into my lane. Until, that is, the honking from behind became unbearable. Can I ever get it right?

After the centre of Andorra, the traffic eased, the rain stopped and the clouds began to lighten. Might there be a chance that I could after all enjoy myself climbing up to the Col de Puymorens that marks the border with France? Only thirty minutes ago I had not dared dream about it. The closer I came to the end of Andorra (the city, as opposed to the country), however, the more promising the situation looked. I could see mouth-watering serpentines in the distance. And some of the far-away hills were even lit up with spots of sunlight. There was by now only one thing between me and some serious driving: that tiny Peugeot 205CTI that I had let merge in a while ago.

While I had barely noticed him before, I now took an instant dislike to him, because what stood out was a long catalogue of tiny differences. To start, his was a humble Peugeot, mine a classy Aston Martin. It sported – what a joke! – a couple of racing stripes and a bigger exhaust pipe. If my friend's Aston had sported stripes and a bigger exhaust pipe, what with that coming on top of Rothsay Red and ivory interior, I would have had to forego a chance to drive it. The driver was young, muscular and tall and he almost hit the roof lining with his head. I am, well, old, scrawny, and short, short enough in fact to leave nigh-on a foot of clearance between my head and the car's roof lining. He wore sunglasses even though the clouds had only just begun to lift. I, instead, like to look people in the eye, and so never wear sunglasses, not even in the height of the Australian summer. (Really dumb, that, by the way.) There was only one redeeming feature in that CTI driver, and it was this: when he looked in the rear view mirror, I detected at times a corner-of-the-mouth smirk which alternated with a hint of a smile.

Now, you must understand, over the years, I have built up a database of associations in my head that links automotive and behavioural clues to experiences with fellow drivers. Here is what my database told me about this 205. Being black and having stripes and a bigger exhaust pipe told me that there would likely be an element of aggression in his behaviour. The fact that it was a neglected car with a few dents meant that the car had been worked hard. The CTI in the equation meant that the owner had probably bought the most powerful 205 he could afford. That, in turn, meant that he'd enjoy driving fast, for what

"What a joke!"

other reason is there to buy a CTI? It could also have been because the CTI looked cooler and slicker, but I rejected this hypothesis because his car was suffering, as I said, from acute neglect. And people who love cars for their cool and slick looks tend not to neglect them.

As for the driver himself, his continually ogling me meant that he treasured my car because mine – well, alright, my friend's – was the kind of car he would buy if the sun of life shone on him. In fact, his smirk told me something else. I bet he was thinking to himself: "Look at this. Another rich old fogey, with poor taste, but the money to afford a car like that. Shame that he probably doesn't know how to drive it." In other words, he was contemplating life's fundamental injustice: why is it always that the people who have the most seem to deserve it the least? An entirely human thought, is it not? And his next thought was almost certainly this: "If I had a car like yours, it would actually be driven the way it was meant to be!"

What about the fact that he was driving at the speed limit and kept a big distance between him and the cars ahead until they had all disappeared? It perfectly completed the puzzle. He was creating the space to prove that he'd be a more deserving driver of the Aston Martin than I. And the final clue: he was local and so knew the roads.

All this added up to one gigantic, ominous difference (0.0001%, in fact) and my not liking this guy one bit. Except for that hint of a smile. What did it add up to? I was about to find out.

When we were well out of Andorra City and the first serpentine came into view at the end of a pretty much straight section, the CTI suddenly bolted forward. For a second, I was tempted to let him go, as I had the motorbike earlier that day, because this wasn't my car and the chances of me coming to like him were practically nil, but his faint smile continued to intrigue me. So, I threw caution to the wind, shifted down, and leaped forward as well. In that first serpentine, the CTI-owner took me by surprise. He slowed down a lot harder than I expected and practically threw the car into the turn, wheels squealing and screeching. Wow, that guy really means business, I thought to myself.

Alright then, since there was nothing coming as far as I could see, I whipped the Aston through the turn too – not very gentlemanly, that! On the following straight, I took advantage of my Vantage to make up for lost ground. In fact, by the middle of that straight run I had recovered from my surprise and was ready to pass him: my car was simply that much faster. But then I asked myself: How meaningful is this? I mean, it goes without saying that a 420 horsepower twelve-cylinder will outrun a car with one quarter of that power any time. In fact, if I passed him on a straight, it would only have proved his point: all the old fogey knows is how to open the throttle.

So, I resolved to hang with him in the next turn, which is what I did. We went through the next turn from side to side via the apex like two figure skaters in a joint act, leaning and working hard to maintain balance. Now it was he who was surprised. He hadn't expected the old fogey to keep up with him, not through the turns that were his back yard. We zoomed through a few more twisties and then caught up with the bevy of slow moving cars that he had let pull away, way back in the city centre.

Now that we had established a bit of mutual respect we moved on to the next phase in our nascent relationship. How would we behave in the presence of third parties?

The first signs were not encouraging. He almost piled into the boot of the first car he ran up against. That wasn't because he misjudged the distance. No, he was simply still determined to stay ahead of me. And so he and I began to look out for openings to pass. But each new turn revealed only short open spaces, too short for passing one car, let alone two at a time. I decided that I would have to let him go first and therefore hung back a bit. That made him relax. While he was still apprehensively surveying the scene for an opportune time to go in for the kill like a cat stalking its prey, he did not attempt to pass until he could clearly see that there was space to do it right. That assured me in my belief, prompted first by his smile, that I was after all not dealing with a lunatic, just with a rather spirited driver.

Eventually an opening to pass came. He didn't need to shift down; he just whisked his car out as soon as he spotted the opening and accelerated as hard as the CTI would permit, which wasn't very fast, however, since we were going uphill. I held back, figuring that if he encountered on-coming traffic he would need space to fall back into line. Nothing came, so he successfully passed the first car. Then more openings appeared. When he went on to nab the second car, I passed the first. Then he the third and I the second, and so on until the bevy was behind us. To mutual respect for fundamental skills had been added a shared sense of reasonableness.

This left open one more question: would the initial jabbing of jaws escalate into fierce biting or relax into joyful play? Would we end up antagonists or friends?

Before the final ascent to the Col de Puymorens, there is a longer stretch of reasonably straight road. Once again, I approached him with the total might of the DB7, fully expecting to let him stay in front because, as I said: what would have been the point of passing him on a straight? To my surprise, however, he switched on his right turn signal as I approached, clearly indicating, "Hey buddy, I know your car's faster than mine – and you're not quite the old fogey I imagined you to be – so, have at it. Go ahead and pass!"

While I had, until now, resisted the temptation to pass him on the straights, now I obliged. In fact, this was important, because if I did not, I would have snubbed a courtesy, which would have tightened the tension instead of relaxing it.

And so I passed him, but not without looking over and seeing a pronounced smile which I reciprocated in spades. I pulled away from him for a little while only to relax back into a comfortable pace. He was with me again in less than a few seconds. By slowing down a bit I signalled to him, "Look, my friend, that was great, but enough's enough." He picked up this signal of mine, but couldn't help pass me in turn. After he had done so, he too relaxed into a comfortable pace.

A short while later, we reached the Col de Puymorens. Both of us had emerged from a sweaty workout and, with the rushing away of one cloud, stepped into the sunny, mountainous splendour that is the Pyrenees.

Even though we still had not spoken a word, we could both tell that we felt great. This was a relationship a lot rowdier than the gentlemanly encounter of mid-day. For all that rowdiness, it felt even better because, instead of falling instantly into place, it was one to which the outcome wasn't clear at the start. There is something special about the circuitous fulfilment of anticipation, as if the anticipation is heightened with every twist and every turn. I did not expect him to drive as well as he did; nor did I expect him to be as circumspect and generous of mind in the end. He teased and tempted me to think of him in one way, but in the end forced me to throw away my earlier preconceptions. I expected resolution to lay this way and then that, almost like in a good thriller. In the end, it emerged that our driving styles fitted each other to perfection, against all the odds.

From the top of the pass, we continued driving together toward Aix-les-Thermes and eventually Toulouse where we parted company. On the way, we grabbed each other as we swung through turns, seemingly enjoined by an invisible cord. We tugged each other to higher speed and jabbed at each other in momentary bursts of acceleration. We flashed our lights in mutual acknowledgement. We jumped over bumps. At times, he ran ahead; at others he fell behind and then caught up. We approached and evaded each other in bouts of mock-attack. Despite the tiny differences that loomed so large at the start, all this took place, not in competition, but in joyful play made possible by the silent communication of two kindred spirits.

CHAPTER SIX

Companionship

"I have found out that there ain't no surer way to find out whether you like people or hate them than to travel with them." – Mark Twain.

I still recall the moment as if it was yesterday. I was standing a few feet away from my car, yet could still hear, faintly, the crackling of its engine and piping. I always love that sound for it speaks of healthy exhaustion; if sweating gave off a sound, this would be it. I was absorbed by a black, ragged mountain range's reflection on the still lake before me and took in the sun's last few warming rays as she sank beyond those mountains, robbing them of texture and depth and leaving behind only their silhouettes. Already, there was mist rising for without the sun the air was freezing, beckoning the lake to surrender some of the warmth it had horded throughout summer. I stood motionless and gazed. I don't recall for how long. The majesty of the moment had stopped time. Suddenly, the breaking up of a flock of birds restarted time, and I thought, it must be late: I must be going. I looked at my watch and was surprised. It was only 4 in the afternoon. But then I remembered that the sun sets early here, in this part of Bavarian Germany, near Kochel am See: it was late October and daylight saving time was no more.

I had been driving all afternoon from Lake Constance along the German Alpenstrasse (Route of the Alps) on this last day of my holiday. With no goal but a desire to make the best of this splendid fall day, I had taken off four hours earlier, accompanied by nothing except a map. What a perfect day for driving it had been. Up above, the sky was ice blue. Still-green meadows were aplenty. I spotted occasional patches of snow, remnants of prematurely wintry days. And wherever I looked, there were trees turning bright yellow, rich orange and deep red. Better yet, I was driving on roads of all shapes and arrangements: straights along lakes, sweeping bends across hilltops, and tight turns of every orientation. I felt surge after surge of exhilaration, all while being immersed in this natural splendour. I wanted to etch these sensations and scenes into my memory so that I could recall them at will. But there was also something else. I wanted to share them with someone.

I drove on toward Mittenwald and then Innsbruck in Austria. The snowy mountain peaks of the Karwendel, a mountainous nature reserve to the northeast of the Olympic town, lit up in sparkling pink, then purple and, at last, lilac. Day had become night. I was overwhelmed with feelings. If only I could share with someone what I had seen and what I had experienced today, driving with abandon through landscape like this. Men really are losers when it comes to being alone. We just can't do it.

Now, whether you agree with me or not that making friends out of strangers is hard, surely you will agree that finding a soul mate for life is infinitely harder. First, small differences not only loom large, they actually drive you crazy. In fact, it's not the small differences such as whether you believe in god or whether children are cheaper by the dozen. Not at all. These things are sorted in no time. Instead, what really gets you is differences like this: she wants to cuddle at night when you want nothing but peace and quiet; he wants to cuddle in the morning when she's dead to the world. Or, even more ominous, she thinks nothing of running around barefoot in the depth of winter while he keeps his socks on at the height of summer. Two people with feet that are never at the same temperature, that can spell disaster.

To the problems arising from the tiniest of differences must be added the amount of seemingly futile but somehow highly effective deception that is employed during the early stages of dating. His parting dropping more and more to one side in a vain attempt to make-believe that he's got more hair than he really does. Or her wearing Styrofoam-lined bra cups that scream out loud, "Tiny boobs ahead!"

So, a sure test must be found that will indicate, without a trace of doubt, whether two people are made for one another. I can't think of a better one than driving thousands of miles together before tying the knot.

At any rate, I was dreaming about an ever-lasting companion. It turned out that I would be dreaming for a long time before my dream was eventually fulfilled. Coming to the realisation that reality is rarely like a dream, on the other hand, was swifter. What should have tipped me off was this: I am a terrible passenger. I don't trust anyone else when it comes to driving.

This is why I never quite got this story about a perfect example of blind trust. A young couple were going on a driving holiday the day that she picked up her driving licence. They left early in the afternoon. For the first thirty minutes, he drove on the broad boulevards that led away from their home town. Just before a "winding road ahead" sign, he pulled over and, coming to a halt, suggested, "How about you drive?"

There was a moment's hesitation for she knew what awaited her on the narrow mountain roads ahead. It was Friday afternoon and 18-wheel trucks were all in a rush to make it home before the weekend trucking curfew. And, surely, her partner would be unable to curb either his impatience or his opinions. Still, she was a confident lady and said, "Sure!" They both got out of the car. She walked around to the driver's side and hopped in. Her friend walked around as well, but instead of getting in beside her, opened the rear door, got in and lay down on the back seat. "I'm taking a nap," he said yawning. And off she drove.

I never got it. I still don't get it. How can anyone have so much trust in somebody else's driving?

* * *

My wife and I met in Hong Kong. I took instant notice when, after a dinner with friends, she not only ordered a glass of port, but also lit up a fine Cuban cigar. Before the evening was out, I was in love and kissed her hand when we parted. I know now that at that time she said to herself: "This must be an Austrian thing!" To this day, she swears that the possibility that I might have fallen head-over-heel in love with her never occurred to her. And so she held out for a very long time.

Was it only me who could see that this relationship was made in heaven, so entirely unlike the typical man-woman relationship? Not long before I had heard that it had been scientifically proven that men liked pretty, young, and faithful women, and that women liked rich, ambitious, and older men. There is nothing so typical about us. For example, she doesn't like shopping and I don't watch television. How typical is that? But then I took a closer look at the two of us. My wife-to-be was attractive and youthful and I, well, I drove a Porsche, still faster than anyone else, and, if you recall, had long ago given a new meaning to the term pattern baldness. Point taken.

Our relationship took off in Milano. We met there on a lovely September day, at the end of a holiday for her and a business trip for me. We planned to drive from Milano to Salzburg and stay there a few days. Could it get any more romantic? Could it get any better? It was a driving holiday made in heaven and exactly what I had been dreaming about.

"Darling, can you please park straight," my companion suggested.

"Park straight? What do you mean? I am parked straight!" I replied.

"No, I don't think so. Just have a look." She tried to convince me.

"I am looking, dear, I am. And I am parked straight," I insisted.

It was our first argument, and it continued for a while until we discovered that we were both right. She had based her claim about my crooked parking on the orientation of the car parked next to us. In relation to it, she was right: I wasn't parked straight. I, on the other hand, was referring to my car's alignment with the markings on the ground. In relation to those, I was parked perfectly straight. Same situation, different points of view. That was a great lesson about preventing small differences from growing up and looming large. Surely

"Same situation, different points of view..."

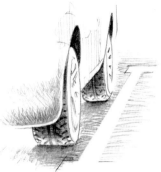

it would be all smooth sailing from here on out, so long as we kept this fundamental insight in mind.

The route from Milano to Salzburg is straight forward and all highway: Milano, Bergamo, Brescia, Verona, Trento, Bolzano, Innsbruck, Rosenheim, Salzburg. Approximately 350 kilometres of smooth cruising. But I wouldn't be caught dead doing that. If it had been up to me, I would've stretched this drive into a 700 kilometre Alpine roller coaster. However, I was mindful that this was our maiden car journey, so I would not do what I was thirsting to do. No, not at all, I was going to be entirely respectful and considerate. In this spirit I suggested only a short winding detour, namely that after Bergamo we'd drive along the Lago d'Iseo, wind our way over the Passo del Tonale and then pick up the highway again in Bolzano. And my sweet darling consented.

I took the highway exit at Castelli Calepio and the first words I heard were these:

"Oh, darling, please, not so close."

"Close to what?" I was about to say, but caught myself in time, and replied instead, "Yes, dear," and fell back a few hundred meters. This was going to be painful.

The scenery along the western side of Lago d'Iseo is fantastic, what with towering Monte Isola plainly visible in the middle of the lake. Since I was crawling at a snail's pace – not on account of traffic; no, it was just that I had already concluded that the journey toward shared driving pleasures was going to take a while – my companion felt entirely comfortable to take in the landscape and relish the drive.

Suddenly she went, "Oh, look! From up there we'd have a beautiful view!" She was pointing to a hill on our left and a road that led up to it. Now, if there is one thing I've always prided myself in, it was that I could make any turn, even at the last minute. So, I threw a glance in the rear view mirror, flicked on the blinker, and turned left.

"You just scared the living daylights out of me! Where are we going?" was my companion's flustered response.

"But, darling, you just said that you'd like to take a look from up there, no?" I tried to justify my accomplished driving.

"Oh, sweetheart, that's very considerate of you. You really know how to surprise me!" she replied in beautifully diplomatic language. And then added: "I know how well you drive; you don't need to show me."

The second useful lesson for life and for driving: surprises are the anathema of passengers. And lesson number three: my wife, then as much as now, likes being driven the way she likes being served in a restaurant: the more inconspicuous the better.

At any rate, we continued on our way up to the lookout she had spotted. It took us to a little town called Vigolo and from there the view of Lago d'Iseo, dotted with white sail boats and dominated by Monte Isola, was indeed spectacular. We parked our car near the sanctuary of the Madonna di Loreto, got out and walked around for a while through Vigolo's narrow alleys and arched passageways. Right around the time when I was ready to go again, my companion surmised, "What a beautiful place! How about staying a little while longer? We can go back to the car, roll down the windows, and sit and talk for a while." Talk? I wanted action and she wanted to develop our relationship. Men are from Mars, and women from Venus.

Before long, we did resume our drive. For a while the road from Lago d'Iseo toward Bolzano was reasonably straight. But as we approached the Passo del Tonale, the winding sections increased. So did the audible gasps of my companion. In one particular turn the gasps turned into a faint scream. I felt so sorry, especially since I could tell that it was entirely involuntary. She had tried her mighty best to contain it.

"I don't want to tell you that you're driving too fast for my liking!" she said sweetly.

"Yes, it's a bit disturbing!" I agreed.

So what should we do? We thought about it for a while. As it turned out, a little bit of relationship building did the trick. She promised to tap my shoulder instead of making noises whenever she became uncomfortable. And I promised to slow down in response to this signal. Now this worked pretty well. Of course, most of the time she tapped me on my shoulder way before I thought she'd be uncomfortable, but it was a huge improvement over the sorry wails that it replaced.

"A little bit of relationship building did the trick..."

So, we drove deeper into the afternoon. By the time we were following the sweeping turns leading up to the Brennero that divides Italy and Austria, the sun was setting. It reminded me of that beautiful late afternoon drive when I was all alone. The Alps had been lit up by the glorious rays of the setting sun, then as much as now. Meanwhile, my loved one had fallen asleep. I wasn't sure whether to be sad again about not being able to share the beauty of the moment as I had wished all along, or be relieved because I was able to drive without interruption once more.

Later that evening we arrived safe and sound in Salzburg. It was, all in all, a wonderful day and a memorable driving tour, the first of many, many more to come. And so we went on to a little more relationship building. That was a good thing, because worse was to come.

* * *

The day of our engagement was both the best and the worst. I took my fiancée-to-be on a morning drive that ended at Birnau, a beautifully restored baroque church overlooking Lake Constance. She was surprised when I suggested we attend mass. This is because she knows I'm not much for attending mass, so she found this rather touching, especially since it was Whitsunday. After mass, in the lovely May sun and among the vines of the convent's vineyard, I proposed. Her response was as untraditional as it was ambiguous: "Of course!" This made me wonder: of course, what? "Yes, of course!"? Or, "Of course not!"? It wasn't until I saw her warm smile that I was reasonably certain.

After lunch, we took off on our driving holiday as planned, now happily engaged as husband-and-wife-to-be. Our destination was Lake Annecy, in France, just south of Geneva. We drove along the foothills of the Alps first by Zürich and then by Bern, marvelling at the beauty of Switzerland's picturesque landscape, dotted as it is with chalet-like houses whose balconies and window sills overflowed with blooming potted plants, just as they do every spring and every summer. Not long after Bern and then Fribourg, the highway descended through sweeping bends and revealed for the first time the crescent-shaped Lac Leman and the outline of Europe's highest mountain, Mont Blanc. At Vevey, we turned left unto the highway that leads south past Montreux to Martigny. We were once again in the midst of vineyards. My fiancée loved the moment because it put her right back to where I had proposed earlier that day. She also very much enjoyed the lack of highway excitement. All in all, the world couldn't have been finer for her.

I thought so too, except that to me the near-straight highway was rather dull. So, my anticipation rose with every kilometre that we got closer to Martigny because it was there that we would exit the highway and I could begin to have some fun on the back roads to Annecy.

I knew those roads very well. Immediately after leaving the highway in a suburb of Martigny called Bourg, the road rises up along a few snaking bends. Then, there is a 180 degree turn. From there the road just keeps on rising, pretty much straight for a while, until it hits a number of serpentines, which eventually culminate in the Col de la Forclaz. As I entered the bottom of this playground, I saw in the distance a few cars, including a crawling bus. That gave me extra incentive to make the most out of that first 180 degree turn. I zoomed up through the sweeping bends, and slowed down hard while simultaneously hugging the right-hand side of the road, from where a steep slope fell away. The road was clear for as far as I could see. I shifted down, turned in, and aimed at the apex. From the apex, I accelerated with all the might of my car's engine and let myself be carried back out to the far end of the turn as I shifted up. It was then that I noticed a sharp pain in my shoulder. I had completely forgotten about my fiancée.

"Was that really necessary?" she wanted to know.

"I am so sorry, honey! I don't know what's gotten into me." In truth, I knew very well: I just wanted to gobble up this road.

"At least, if you're going to do that, let me know ahead of time, would you, please?" she requested.

"Of course, I will from now on." Then, to distract her, I added, "Look, how beautiful it is here."

"Mm Hmmm," was her ominous reply.

A bit further up the road we caught up with the little platoon of cars, led by a bus pensively enveloped in its own exhausts. My fiancée's instinct, as that of the other drivers queuing up behind the bus, was to close the vents, sit back, relax and enjoy the scenery. My instinct, on the other hand, was to pass and put this stinking polluter behind us.

I've always loved passing on back roads. My finest enjoyment is when I look ahead and see only a few more cars coming, after which there is a stretch of road with no on-coming traffic. Exactly as it was then. It perfectly heightened my anticipation. While the remaining on-coming cars filed by me, I shifted down, flicked on the turn indicator and slowly closed in on the cars to be passed. All the while, my heartbeat was ramping up because I could feel the shove of acceleration long before I made it happen. And then there it was. The last car had passed. I opened the throttle and pulled out onto the left lane. In deference to my fiancée's wishes, I also cried, in the very last second, "I'm going to pass!"

With one hand she held on to her seat, with the other to my shoulder. Her whole body stiffened; living body turned in an instant into cadaver. There was nothing to be done at that moment, however, so I kept going since hesitation is not a good idea when passing other cars. After successfully overtaking the bus, I pulled back into my lane. I felt I needed to say something.

"But, darling, I did tell you that I was going to pass," I tried to explain.

"Not good enough!" came the reply.

There was silence for a while. She was clearly thinking because it was obvious to her that the question of how to drive harmoniously together ranked pari passu with the question of whether we would eventually have children or whether we needed to take along one or two toothbrushes on holidays. It was a question of immense importance.

After a while, she pronounced her verdict.

"You are not giving me a choice!"

"Oh, sweetie, I am so sorry. It won't happen again."

"Don't sweet-talk me, mate. Just involve me in what you're doing. That will do just fine."

That actually made some sense. During our friendship I had taken very few potentially life-threatening (from her point of view) actions without first getting her opinion. So, I resolved to tell her earlier. In fact, I'd do better than that: I'd actually ask for her approval. Now this sounds rather draconian, but in fact, it worked pretty well because she has never asked for a form filled out in triplicate when I wanted to hug a corner or pass a few cars. No, a simple, "The road is free up-ahead. Are you ok if I pass?" has ever since always elicited a smile and, in 99 cases out of a 100, a nod. This then, was lesson number four.

However, at that moment, I didn't yet know all that, so my attempt to involve her was rather clumsy. That is, I asked her whether she'd be ok to read the map and be my co-pilot. And I could use her help because I wasn't as sure about the road from Chamonix to Annecy as I was about the previous stretch.

"Darling, Chamonix is coming up just down the road. Can you help figure out where we need to go?"

"Okay!" she beamed and proceeded to unfold the map.

She pored over the map for a while and then gave me directions. For the rest of the trip, she was the navigator and I began to practise involving her in other ways. "How about this?" "How about that?" This seemed to work pretty well until about ten kilometres before Annecy where she suddenly cried in alarm, "Pull over! Now!"

Which I duly did. As soon as I came to a stop, she popped open the door and threw up. What she had forgotten, and I never knew, was that reading a map made her sick. Lesson number five: don't leave home without motion sickness pills.

A little while later we arrived at Auberge du Pere Bise, a place we had decided to splurge on to celebrate our engagement. Unfortunately, my wife-to-be was not only still sick from the winding roads, but had also swollen eyes from an attack of hay fever. Instead of enjoying the delicacies of old Pere Bise – something she had been looking forward to as much as becoming engaged to me – she went straight to bed. We had clearly reached a new low-point in our relationship.

By the next morning all was forgiven, however. We were planning to head South all the

way to Provence on all but straight roads. Still, our first stop that day was at a pharmacy where we bought a copious amount of pills against *mal de voyage*, just in case.

We arrived sooner than we thought. It was early afternoon. Soon we would be at our destination for the day, St. Remy de Provence. We remembered that we needed to leave the A7 at Cavaillon, a name I and my wife had hitherto associated with juicy, sweet melons. (We can't help being surprised, time and again, when it turns out that some food or drink we like – Camembert is one, Champagne another – is actually the name of a place.) At the juicy melon exit, we turned west onto the D99. For a moment, we were tempted to turn east and drive past Cavaillon into the Luberon, just for the afternoon, to refresh fond memories that had been placed and securely fastened in our minds by Peter Mayle, that master of the well-placed bon mot, in *A Year in Provence, Hotel Pastis* and *A Dog's Life*. Our memories of the Luberon are vivid. Shame that we had yet to visit.

Not that time either. On our Michelin map, the D99 looked dead straight for long sections, but was nonetheless highlighted in green to promise scenic beauty. We wondered what it had in store for us. At first, we didn't see much, only a few non-descript, dirty-beige houses on both sides, a far cry from what our implanted memories of Provence had made us expect. We settled into listless driving and began to wonder whether perhaps Mayle's Luberon existed only in his imagination. But just then, after passing the intersection with the N7, we couldn't believe our eyes. Our hearts jumped. There, on both sides of the road, were massive trees with ponderous, grey-black pillars reaching toward the sky, their leafy canopies embracing each other as if to make the roof of a magnificent gothic cathedral. We entered this place of automotive worship and were instantly in awe at its splendour. Thank heavens, the road was as straight as if drawn with a ruler. This gave us the leisure to let our eyes wander from the cathedral's floor to its ceiling and from side to side, the better to absorb the interplay between nature's beauty and man's arrangement.

As we drove on, we were also fascinated by the intricacy of the brocade pattern on the road itself, created by the early afternoon sun filing through the cathedral's porous roof-top. We were struck, too, not by the pattern's permanence, but by its sway as the wind tousled the leaves overhead. The straightness of the road allowed our minds to wander. It all was so beautiful that we, like Peter Mayle, wanted to share with others what we saw as supreme beauty. But then we wondered: should we? He wrote passionately about his Luberon, but surely as much by a desire to share its beauty with others as by an ad man's instinct for profit, and wound up being attacked for having contributed to the Luberon losing the very charm that had inspired him to pick up his pen in the first place. It prompted us to feel once again the pull of one of life's dilemmas. If one believes firmly, as we do, that no one has the right to tell others what to do or to think, how do we go about sharing this very belief?

Our thoughts flowed freely, encouraged by the ceaseless brushing by of trees along this dead straight road. We hoped it would not end. It was the perfect first glimpse of how beautiful driving together could be.

In fact, our engagement day was the low-point in our automotive relationship. From that day onward, we began enjoying driving together more and more. Of course, on occasion, we still ran into trouble, but most of these incidents were minor. In fact, they were more the source of hilarity than frustration. For example, a few days later on that same trip we were on our way from Perpignan to Carcassonne in the South East of France. We were heading west on the D117 when we came across a sign, just before St. Paul-de-Fenouillet, that pointed us toward the spectacular scenery of the Gorges de Galamus. Since I had by now internalised all the lessons and my dear was drugged on motion sickness pills, she offered, "Why not take the scenic route?" And so we did, with her acting as the navigator once again.

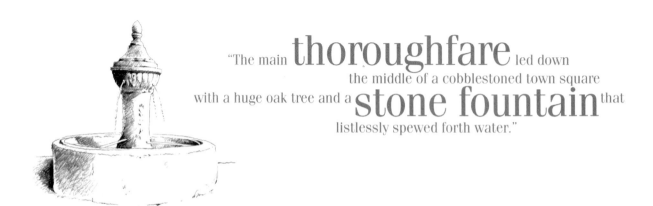

"The main thoroughfare led down the middle of a cobblestoned town square with a huge oak tree and a stone fountain that listlessly spewed forth water."

St. Paul-de-Fenouillet itself was nearly deserted. The main thoroughfare led down the middle of a cobblestoned town square with a huge oak tree and a stone fountain that listlessly spewed forth water. Even though there was no one around, we rolled slowly across the square. I, for one, have always loved driving on cobblestones. There is something comforting about the rumble, tumble and rattle, reminiscent of very different times. And right there in St. Paul-de-Fenouillet, we did feel out of place and time in our flashy car. A corpulent lady watering the potted plants on her balcony looked up, stared for a while and then waved at us as if we were the first foreigners she had ever seen.

The road along the Gorges de Galamus is breath-taking, literally. It is cut into the rock, mostly single-lane and as winding as an audio tape that has come off its spool. When we reached the end of the Gorges at Cubieres-sur-Cinoble, my navigator said, "Turn left." But my gut feeling told me right, so I over-ruled her. About an hour later we both simultaneously recognised the same rotund lady we had seen watering her plants. She waved at us again with an expression that blended surprise and pity to perfection.

Final lesson: don't over-rule a competent navigator. Still, we had to smile. And we got to see the Gorges one more time. From here on in, it was really all smooth sailing.

* * *

Our very first, thoroughly enjoyable driving holiday took us to Scotland, all the way from Austria. On the evening before we were due to leave, we were having dinner with good friends. Full of anticipation, we talked about what we expected to see and how much we were longing to go on this vacation. Toward the end of a typical Austrian desert – Marillenknödel – we saw the moon rising over the hills, rubbing its eyes gently. It was enough for my now-wife to suggest: "How about we leave right now instead of tomorrow morning? It's such a beautiful night. Are you up for it?" Am I up for it? Is the pope catholic?

We excused ourselves, went home and grabbed our bags, which were all packed since we had intended to leave early the next morning. Within 45 minutes we were on the German highway leading north from Lake Constance. By then, the moon was fully awake and the stars were out in full brightness. The scented early September air coming in through our open sunroof suffused the compartment with the spices of autumn. For quite a while we drove without talking. The moonlight was milky and diffuse and gave the hilly landscape of southern Germany a ghostly appearance, both sharply delineated and eerily vague.

We had chosen the route via Germany (Stuttgart, Karlsruhe, Frankfurt, Aachen) because we could drive faster which would more than make up for the longer distance. (The shorter route is to drive through France.) By the time we had settled into our cruising speed, the wind noise was becoming bothersome. We closed the sunroof and put on our favourite night-driving music, some pop (Bhudda Bar) and some Jazz (Joe Sample). Eventually, my wife dug deeper into our collection and pronounced, "How about this? It seems appropriate." She had somehow found Beethoven's Moonlight sonata. It was a leftover from a time when I first enjoyed listening to classical music because of its heart-rending romance, but also

"The moonlight was milky and diffuse
and gave the hilly landscape a
ghostly appearance..."

because it made me feel rather sophisticated for claiming I knew something about it. And she was right. This was splendid music for the occasion. By the time we were on the third track, the presto finale, wow, what a surprise! Did Beethoven anticipate powered transport? Or even the pleasure of driving under a bright moon? Perhaps he had only a horse-drawn carriage at full speed in mind, but some sort of driving he must have been dreaming about.

And so we kept going north and further north until Aachen, which we reached well past midnight. There we turned left. Well, not exactly, we turned right and a jug handle took us around and around until we were going west. I warned my dear well ahead that I could use a bit of adrenalin to help me stay awake for the rest of the night. For once, her concern for our safety actually made her want me to go faster. So we zoomed through 270 degrees of a merry-go-round to the sound of deep-in-the-night laughter and giggles.

In Belgium, we slowed down a bit and opened up the sunroof again. Our companion, the moon, was still with us. In fact, it accompanied us all through the night. Wherever we went, it was with us. At times, it illuminated the road ahead; at others, it appeared, disappeared and reappeared in our rear view mirrors.

By 4:30am we had reached Calais and were checking into the Channel Tunnel train. We were fortunate because the next train was due shortly. Thank heavens; if we had had to sit there for long we would both have fallen asleep in the queue.

After boarding the train, I suggested that we get out and stretch our legs. My wife would have none of it, however. "Let's stay right here, in our car, our home away from home!" Those were her last words before she dozed off. Meanwhile, I sat there by myself, giddy with excitement from the past few hours' drive and the holiday that had just started. Sitting there in my car that was moving yet not moving, I reflected on what an engineering achievement the Chunnel has been. Not that I would want to trade driving for sitting in a train. Still, I was almost filled with envy when we reached Dover because one moment the train was moving,

"What a consummate transition: one **moment** the train was **moving,** the next it was not."

the next it was not, but I couldn't tell when. What a consummate transition. I don't think I could ever do it so well.

My wife woke up shortly before we arrived at our friend's place in London, just in time for breakfast. Rarely have I seen her relate a driving experience so vividly…almost as if she had been sound asleep and with sweet dreams all night long.

* * *

Two days later we continued, driving north toward Scotland. By 7am we were on the M1. We got up early in order to beat the morning traffic. Our plan for that day was to go north, far north, to get as close as we could to the Isle of Skye. The route was straightforward. We would stay on the M1 to Birmingham, there turn onto the M6 to Carlisle, then the M74 to Glasgow. That would be all highway. From Glasgow to Fort William, we'd be on the A82. We didn't think we'd make it much further. My wife had studied the route, folded up the map and placed it next to her seat. "You will stop when nature calls, right? I'll give you plenty of warning." With that she fell into silence. And so we drove, for a couple of hours, both of us preoccupied with our own thoughts.

It is a bit depressing around here, was a thought that bubbled up around Manchester and Liverpool, for almost all that we saw along the highway were the pockmarks of industrialisation. And the tightening and lowering of rain clouds made it worse.

"We will never get there!" my wife sighed.

"Darling, we've only been on the road for a couple of hours. We will, we will," I assured her.

"It's not that. I mean our house: when do you think we will buy one?" she corrected me.

"I am looking forward to it, you know. But I'd really rather build one from scratch, so it can be ours, like none that we'd buy ever could," I explained.

"So you still want to build one, eh? It'll take time, a long time…" She sighed, and then there was silence again.

Preston, then Lancaster. The clouds lifted and so did our mood.

"Whether we build it or not, darling, it must be airy, and bright. I love to wake up to the morning sun, as you know," I continued.

"Don't I ever," she mumbled to herself as we passed one of the many signs to the Lake District, which prompted a happier thought. "And there must be a lake," she suggested. "We must see a lake or the ocean from our house, preferably from our bedroom."

By the time we reached Glasgow, we'd gone through every room in our house, from the outdoor shower – a must – to the kitchen and the cigar divan, from our wine cellar to two studies, a mansion by any other name - if we could ever afford it. Past Glasgow, the wide-open spaces of the lowlands gradually gave way to the nooks and crannies of the highlands and, with that, our conversation became more detailed.

"I'm shorter than you, you know," my wife offered up for no apparent reason.

"Yes, I do, but not to worry, my darling, it's your personality that I love."

"No, that's not what I mean. We will need the kitchen counters to be at different heights if you are ever to make good on your promise to start cooking."

Ah, right. And so our conversation continued. With nothing waiting for us except the road ahead and with no schedule to dictate our pace, we were free to give time to each other on the way to Scotland. In fact, we were startled by how much progress we made, not just on the road, but with our house design. We had talked about our house many times before: in our apartment or in a restaurant over dinner, for example. But we always got stuck. Yet that day, when we were driving for hours, the stimuli of our constantly changing surroundings moved our conversation along. All that was missing was a big, heavy ashtray and two fat cigars.

In the late afternoon, we suddenly remembered that our friends had packed us a basket of food. Prompted by the falling sun's sparkling rays over Lochan nah-Achlaise on Rannoch Moor, we pulled over near a big rock and spread out our friend's gifts: everything from marble to raisin cake, Granini fruit juices, marmalade and dented scones. We sat there for a while, looking into the shimmering loch and the swaying tall grass, then packed up and completed our journey to Fort William where we stayed overnight.

In the morning, we woke to rain again and ground-hugging clouds. Never mind. We were told that the clouds would clear before long. After a leisurely breakfast, we stuffed our belongings into our car – every item's place figured out over years of experience. We continued north along Loch Lochy. By the time we reached Invergarry and Loch Garry, the clouds had indeed lifted and rays of sunlight danced on the loch. The road here is set among shapely hills in parts and flanked by marshes and moors in others. On occasion, the sun – a white porcelain disk behind a curtain of vapour – shone through patches of mist. Once they had all cleared, the many small lochs crisply reflected the azure sky and bright clouds.

The A87, like all other roads we drove on in Scotland, was beautifully maintained. Also,

"We suddenly remembered that our friends had packed us a basket of food…"

it was practically empty. Since the few cars we encountered didn't seem to mind being passed, my wife was encouraged to take control of driving, as it were, by prompting me more than once: "Alright, let's go, clear to pass!" (That really helped since I was driving our left-hand drive car.) To top it off, the A87 offered up any combination of shapes I could desire after nearly two thousand kilometres of highway driving during the past few days. There were long straights in which to let go. It had tight turns, especially before Loch Loyne, that required full concentration. And along Loch Cluanie, I found sweeping bends and even ups-and-downs like in the Alps.

I still recall that unforgettable moment when we were driving on a straight that looked like dropping off into a valley where it met the horizon. At the very instant I made that observation, a fighter jet hurtled by overhead. One second we saw him through our open sun roof, the next he had made a left hand down turn into the valley, but not without letting himself first be carried out and up to the right in a broad, swooping arc. After disappearing into the valley, he eventually reappeared in the distance.

"Wouldn't it be something if we could do something like that?" my wife wondered out loud.

Within a minute, we too had disappeared down into the valley, in a set of motions almost as grand as that of the jet.

At the end of Loch Duich, where a short bridge leads from Dornie to Ardelve, we saw, off to the side, Eilean Donan castle. Its black silhouette against the white water glistening in the evening sun was quite a sight to behold. From there it was only a little further to Kyle of Lochalsh. We crossed the giant bridge that connects the mainland with the Isle of Skye and marvelled at the blueness of the deep water underneath. Finally, we had reached Skye. We continued northwest all the way to Dunvegan and finally Duntulm, both the sites of medieval castles. The latter also marked the northern-most point of our trip.

Our drive to Duntulm was only occasionally interrupted by sheep that made it clear that this was their country and their roads. Aside from watching out for wayward sheep, we could give ourselves entirely to absorbing Scotland's magnificent landscape, dotted as it is with white houses set in primordial, wind-swept landscapes. The wind there makes everything look rugged because it is a wind that never lets up. It bends trees and bushes to grow at sharp angles. And whenever we were parked – in fact, even when we were not – the fierce gusts buffeted our car and shook us within it.

* * *

Scotland was memorable because it was the first trip that I can genuinely say we both enjoyed. Still, there was something missing, because, as you know by now, I am really in my element in winter. Winter is all about sliding, but my wife didn't seem quite ready for that. The few times firm grip faded into skidding on standing water or gravel, I felt her hands on my shoulder in an instant, digging hard, then harder. But eventually there was a break-through.

It was during one unforgettable winter drive from Vienna to Lake Constance when everything fell into place. On that particular occasion, we started out in bright sunshine

from Vienna in our 911, which, in winter, always runs on four soft and gripping snow tyres.

After an hour's drive on the highway toward Salzburg, the wind drew a blanket of clouds across the sky. Then, fifty kilometres before Salzburg, snow began to fall. By the time we passed by Mozart's city, the highway was solidly covered with snow. Inside the car, we listened to music, and we were warm and cosy. Outside, it had turned into deep winter. Just past the Austrian-German border at Salzburg, traffic slowed and the news on the radio let us know that traffic on the notoriously busy stretch from Salzburg to Munich had come to a virtual standstill. When the sun shines and the roads are clear the drive from Salzburg to Lake Constance takes no more than three hours via Munich. Listening to the news, however, we estimated that it would take at least five hours if we stayed on the highway.

Out came the maps. There was a second alternative, namely via a country road from Bad Reichenhall in Germany, the Steinpass to Lofer in Austria and from there, via St. Johann, to Woergel where this winding road joins the highway to Innsbruck, the Arlberg region and, finally, Lake Constance. The options, then, were these: a chance to drive in deep winter on a winding country road or the frustration of being stuck for hours sitting in dense traffic. It was an easy choice for me, but what would my wife have to say? I looked at her with yearning and begging eyes that she could not say no to. And so, I was nervously granted permission to get off the highway.

Snow kept falling heavily and the wind blew fiercely. We were not just in the midst of winter, but in the middle of a snowstorm. Once past Bad Reichenhall, there was hardly a car on the road. Tree branches hung low over the roads, snowdrifts spilled deeply into them, from left and from right. Outside, there was nothing but snow, snow and more snow. Yet inside, here we were, in our Bordeaux-coloured 911, wrapped up in wafts of warm air and the scents of leather. It made my wife forget that snow might be scary. Little did she know that it would take us four hours just to rejoin the highway. But what a fabulous four hours they turned out to be, navigating through turns and bends adrift with snow, sneaking along straights, powering uphill, the rear-end of the 911 wedeling happily. My wife was enthralled with her first drive in winter, for she had never experienced anything quite like it. On one occasion she put her hand on my shoulder – the 911 was at a 45-degree angle coming out of a turn – but for the most part she either leaned into turns along with me or took in the magnificent winter landscape all around us. It left her so impressed that the ginger bread house she baked and decorated with icing sugar that Christmas found its inspiration in the many snow-covered houses we saw, sunk in snow so deep that it stretched seamlessly from the rising hills behind them right onto their roofs. What's more, she came away changed forever by the remarkable discovery that skating – a favourite pastime in her youth – is not only possible on four wheels, but can be beautifully exciting, even for her as a passenger. As for me, it was a day of bliss, because it was pleasure – pure driving pleasure – shared.

"Life...
to skid in broadside,
thoroughly used up,
totally worn out and
loudly proclaiming:
Wow,
what a ride!"

Because it is also an adventure, shared with my

friends.

In life's **darkest** moments,
I prefer to be alone.
In its **brightest**, never.

"Growing old is **mandatory**; growing up is **optional**."

Cheers...

to a laugh and a giggle...
just among ourselves!

CHAPTER SEVEN

Discovery

"The great and recurring question about abroad is, is it worth getting there?"
– Rose Macauly.

After all these years, I still live in Hong Kong. It has grown on me like no other place before, despite the fact that it is rather curious when it comes to cars and driving. While there are driving aficionados in Hong Kong who relish their Sunday morning or late night drives from the southern-most tip of Hong Kong through the heart of the city all the way to the mainland Chinese border – a forty kilometre drive that wets the appetite but never quite satisfies it – in everything from Caterham Super 7s to Lamborghini Murciélagos, most Hong Kongers don't drive their cars, they merely own them. Why? Because, in fact, there is no place to drive. Hong Kongers make up for this by owning as many expensive and fast cars as possible. For example, there are ten times as many Porsche 911s per kilometre of public road in Hong Kong than in Germany. Mercedes Benzes are staple wheels. Rolls Royces are rarer, as one would expect, but they are still quite common. I don't know about you, but my image of a Rolls Royce owner is this: long weekends in Monaco or the like, a chauffeur with hat and white gloves, and the Rolls itself parked in front of the owner's chateau in Scotland. All this is true for Hong Kong's Rolls Royce owners as well, except that the chateau in Scotland is a tiny 1,500sqft apartment in a Hong Kong district called North Point, reachable by Rolls Royce, but also by subway, bus, taxi and double-decker tram. Hong Kong must be the only place on earth where Rolls Royces sport stickers declaring "My other car is a tram."

Whether the car owned is a Rolls, a Porsche or something humbler, few Hong Kongers know the pleasure of hand-washing their car. That is a job reserved for the domestic helpers who listlessly scrub beautiful cars at 7am every morning in Hong Kong's many underground car parks. Poor souls, they are: the helpers, the cars, and the owners.

When they do drive, Hong Kongers drive with the same sense of urgency they display when they want to board their subway, the Mass Transit Railway. They all want to get in or out at the same time. Their traffic and their subway platforms reflect a people gripped by tremendous impatience and a definite fear of being left behind. But there is something else about Hong Kongers: they have a daily craving for, believe it or not, sautéed chicken feet, with their skin, bones and all, but not, thank heavens, their feathers.

And this made me think the other day. Getting along with the oddest of strangers or a spouse is peanuts compared to getting along with aliens (as the U.S. department of immigration endearingly calls folks from abroad). As soon as we make contact, there are big problems, gigantic problems, in fact. These problems arise, possibly, from a lack of understanding, but certainly from profound differences in eating habits. I mean, how can one possibly understand, let alone get along with people who eat chicken feet, with skin, bones and all, or those in other countries who eat raw fish, or steamed monkey brain or stir-fried locust? These are habits that arouse passions, flaming passions that, I am certain, are at the root of nations making war. By way of counter example, who, after all, would declare war on the Italians? No one. Because, we all love pasta. And Pizza.

So what to do? How to bridge the gap between our desire to learn about other people and our aversion to their oh-so-different eating habits? One way would be to go to live (and work) among all the people of the world. That would mean moving house every six months to cover the world's two hundred odd countries and living to be a hundred. Not very practical, that. So what do we do? We go on holidays. To empty beaches and deserted islands, for example, where, guaranteed, we meet someone from home, our neighbour, most probably. If, on the other hand, we go to a resort or join a tour, well, then the supporting cast goes to tremendous lengths to help us avoid being where we actually are: home away from home in the worst possible sense. (The resort operators aren't dumb. They do know one thing: our experiences of a place are most enjoyable if we're not faced with the additional challenge of having to be there.) But if we really want to be there in the interest of learning and bridging the gap, what do we do? I, for one, go driving, in among all the aliens, because driving exposes me first-hand to their thinking and behaviour. When I drive, nothing protects me from raw interactions with the place's inhabitants. I am really there, wherever there is. What I find is sometimes shocking, but always revealing. And, by the by, my understanding of their habits grows and my sniggering at their odd ways becomes less pronounced or disappears altogether. That's been my experience, no matter where I've gone. Here are three poignant examples…

* * *

It was a humid day, as only days in tropical climates can be. The heavens had opened up early that morning and there was no relief in sight. It was 7am and I was driving for the first time in Shanghai. Despite the early hour, my car was in dense, slow-moving traffic on Huai Hai Zhong Road going toward The Bund, the once and once-again posh area by the Huang Pu river.

Electric buses, crammed with people, were so full that I couldn't help but wonder when a passenger would burst through an open window and fall onto the street. In between the buses were Volkswagen Santana taxis in turquoise green, rusty red and white. All of them were honking their horns to get their right of way. (It is curious how the level of development of a country and the number of per-minute hoots on a busy road are inversely related: the more hoots, the less developed the country.) Interspersed among us was the odd official or company car, an Audi here, a Mercedes there. All were black, even their side-windows tinted impenetrably, lest anyone got a glimpse of whatever insalubrious business was being transacted on the backseat.

And bicycles were everywhere. I have only ever seen so many in China. They were not countable; they were a flood and made a remarkable sight. Their wheels were spinning in a blur, their pedals circulating slowly and pensively, legs moving up and down like steam-driven pistons protruding from and retracting into a hollow, fluttering cone of colour. The bicyclists were all shrouded, from their knees up, in hooded raincoats, one red, another yellow, or dark or light blue, or orange, garish green or black, grey or white, no two alike.

The intersection with Mao Ming Road was approaching, and I knew I needed to turn right. But there was a stream of bicyclists on my right, moving in its own lane, as wide as

"And bicycles were **everywhere.** I have only ever seen so many in China…"

one of those for cars. This stream didn't flood or ebb, but was uniform in speed and density.

I recalled stories by *laowai* ("old outsider", a reasonably endearing term for foreigners like me) friends of mine that accidents with bicyclists were problematic, to say the least. The entanglements were invariably acrimonious and long lasting. Yet, I did need to turn. I wondered how to do what I had seen umpteen times before in China: when a car needs to make a right-hand turn, it gives no quarter to bicycles. It simply expresses its intention by flicking on its blinker. Then it turns. I had seen it done again and again. I knew it worked, yet then I wasn't so sure. The intersection approached and there was no way for me to stop and follow my ingrained approach – to let the bicycles pass until there was room to turn – for the river of bicycles would not stop. I felt immense pressure that my trained politeness would be misunderstood, not least by the driver following me whose eyes I sensed drilling into my neck. I knew, I just knew, the honking was coming. There was no choice. I had to turn.

It took almost superhuman will to overcome my fear of retribution. I was about to do what would result in mayhem and loss of licence in any other country: I cut into moving bicycles.

I almost closed my eyes as I turned. The ocean parted and I was in the promised land, on Mao Ming South Road. In the brief interval of time from moving east on Huai Hai Zhong Road to moving south on its perpendicular, what took place was remarkable. All the moving bicyclists, presumably alerted by my blinker, made room for me with consummate bicycling skill, the instant they saw my turn beginning. Some, those far enough behind, slowed down and passed me on the left. Those closer by, abruptly slowed, balancing at a near standstill while I turned. Others yet, those near the front of my car, swerved out in a wide half-circle and kept going. Within the span of ten seconds, I had interrupted the flow of twenty bicycles, no fewer, and behind me the ocean had closed up again. It was a miracle. There was no cursing, no hand-waving, no mean looks, nothing except a shared stoic acceptance on the part of the bicyclists that, in these circumstances, it was alright for might to make right. That was a revelation. Might, I had learned, should not make right. Before driving in Shanghai, I was inclined to dismiss anything else as stupid. Yet here and then, it worked beautifully well. That was an unforgettable lesson that I could not have learned by taking the train or the tram, staying at home or meeting my neighbour on a deserted island. Plus, I think I could get to like such tolerant people, even though they as much as their Hong Kong compatriots lust for chicken feet – skin, bones and all.

* * *

I must admit that I have a love-hate relationship with Germany. At the centre of my emotional confusion lies the country's attitude to rules. Germans are addicted to rules. I

"...skin, bones and all but not, thank heavens, their feathers..."

don't share this addiction. On the other hand, they do rebel – in their own way – against their own rules. And this I rather like.

But let me start with my dislike. What I have found on German roads is that the country's love-affair with rules goes a lot deeper than one might imagine. While in most countries people grudgingly admit that rules are needed – sadly, to protect the considerate many from the inconsiderate few – in Germany rules (traffic laws, that is) need to go a lot further: they also need to protect the many hapless and innocent from the seemingly even more numerous vigilantes.

If Germans love rules, they love bashing rule-breakers even more. Everyone in Germany, or so it seems, can't help but want to be a member of the *Polizei*. Try breaking traffic laws in Germany and see what happens. Long before any official policeman takes notice, you feel the avid eyes of a fellow driver drilling into you. If he or she deems that you must be put into place, they will honk their horns, flash dirty hand signals and, if there is an opportunity, roll down their windows all the better to hurtle insults at you. Just how widespread this vigilantism is is demonstrated by the fact that Germany has, uniquely as far as I know, a set of specific fines for each of the various insults directed at other road users: a visible tongue costs Euro 150; calling somebody a wanker is worth Euro 2,000; being more descriptive "You idiot, you've obviously escaped from an insane asylum!" means Euro 3,000; and the German height of insults, a raised middle finger, will set you back Euro 4,000.

A terribly unpleasant country to drive in then? Well, not really, because there's more to it than that. Looking a bit closer, I've noticed that Germans actually love escaping from their own rules as much as they hope to make others abide by them. As it turns out, this rebellion has two unexpected, but pleasant consequences: for one, Germans still preserve many speed-limit free highways which is their way of letting their hair down, I suppose; and for another, German's desire to break free from their rules finds expression in a widespread love for understatement.

Understatement? You've got to be kidding, is what I hear you say. And in a way you're right: at first glance, understatement and German drivers don't sit together very well. For starters, Germans make some of the most exciting and in-your-face cars in the world – Porsche GT, Mercedes SLR, BMW M5, Audi RS6, need I say more? They then go on to tune them to even greater prowess. And their tuners are almost as famous as the main brands: Ruf, AMG, Alpina, and Abt. These products are often as conspicuous as you'd imagine, and Germans wear them proudly. Cars, it seems, are possessions and a source of pride first. Only incidentally are they means of transport. So where's the understatement?

It's right here: so much tuning goes on under the cover that many of their cars are wolves in sheep's clothing. And then the drivers have fun at the expense of their unsuspecting victims. For example, when you come to a stop at a red light and a Volkswagen van pulls up next to you, get into a launching race only at the risk of being severely embarrassed. That plain-looking van might very well have a big Porsche engine tucked in underneath and leave you sitting in a cloud of smoking tyres.

I will also never forget one incident when I was driving my 911 – not a slouch of a car, now is it? – on the E45 on my way from Munich to Salzburg. Unusually for this stretch of road, the traffic was very light. I settled into a steady 180 kilometres per hour – a comfortable, low-speed, low-altitude cruise, in other words. After a few minutes, a non-descript mid-sized limousine appeared in my rear-view mirror, getting bigger slowly, ever so slowly. The closer he got, the more clearly I saw a broad smile on the driver's face. Nothing threatening, I thought. I figured, well, I don't want to be in your way, so I moved to the right lane to let him pass. He followed me *tout de suite*. Ok, you want to play, that's fine by me, but I don't think it'll last for very long. C'mon, look at what I've got, and then look at your own car! I nudged my speed higher a bit, and he stayed with me, at a pleasant and respectful distance. I pushed a bit higher still, and he was right there again. To make a long story short, by the time I had completely and utterly exhausted what my 911 could give, the guy passed me with ease, smiling all the way (not an arrogant smirk, but a broad happy-as-can-be grin), in his non-descript, but clearly highly tuned car. Yet, I couldn't help but smile myself. Driving in Germany is, in the end, more of a pleasure than a nuisance, what with beautiful roads where one can enjoy speed and drive in the company of people with a great sense of understated humour. Now if I could only get over the fact that they love Blutwurst topped with, of all things, generous helpings of Sauerkraut and sprinkled with the shavings of pigs' toe nails. (Ok, ok, I made this last one up.)

* * *

If we make war on Italy, it won't be because of their pizza, or their pasta, but rather because of how they drive. That's a sentiment I've heard pronounced more than a few times. At the risk of being called nuts, I will admit that I am rather fond of all things Italian, especially when it comes to driving. To start with, I love their roads and have countless fond memories of driving on them.

The sky was as dark-blue as a sapphire, an expensive one, with no imperfections. Even though it was already late September and still quite early in the day, the sun beat down on the road, my car and me. The cypresses, as black as their own shadows, twisted in the wind and contrasted sharply with the country's beige houses and fields. It was my second day in Tuscany, and I was out to have a good romp. I started out in Sinalunga and had already passed Montepulciano, Chianciano, and Sarteana. On my passenger seat was a Touring Club Italiano 1:200,000 map of Tuscany and Umbria. Earlier, I had folded it tortuously to lay bare the roads I wanted to follow. (Why is it that itineraries and the original map folds never, ever coincide?) I carefully picked a combination of whites (for an extra measure of twistiness), yellow-and-greens (for scenic diversions) and reds (for taking a breather).

I was heading south on a trip that would take me in a rough, very rough, semi-circle to Grosseto later that day. I say rough because most Italian roads are rough in the most endearing way. In many parts, there seems to be a law against roads being straight. For a couple of hours now, I had been driving with rapt attention as I chased the ideal line along

the snaking ribbon of tarmac that cut through the ragged landscape and twisted in every possible way. Each turn, of which there were hundreds if not thousands, was a delightful challenge that preoccupied my mind. After about three hours of this, I felt exhausted and at the same time completely refreshed. It was as if by fully engaging a part of my mind on these superb Italian country roads, all other parts were free to relax and unwind.

By noon I was near Pitigliano, pretty much the southern-most point for the day. It looked spectacular and inviting. A small town perched on a plateau, high above cliffs carved out by the river Lente, its houses seemed to grow out of the cliffs, which are riddled with caves cut out of soft limestone. I parked my car in the shade and walked through a maze of medieval streets to find an oasis called Il Tufo Allegro. It was time for lunch.

About three hours later, when the wild boar stew had been enjoyed and sealed off with a double espresso, I re-entered the amusement park that is the collection of Etruscan roads. The double espresso notwithstanding, I felt lazy and in no mood to pursue the pace of the morning's drive. Instead, I meandered along the road and noticed for the first time how all these twists and bends were punctuated by moguls that would be the delight of every passionate skier. These moguls were not potholes that jar and disrupt the joy of driving. Instead, they made the steering wheel perform a playful dance of tiny steps as the front wheels followed the undulating road surface, a bit left, then a wee turn to the right, then left again. My hands, instead of firmly seizing the steering wheel, loosely embraced it, gave it wiggle room, enough to let it flicker, yet not enough to veer off course. Seeing and feeling the wheel rejoice and the car hop, as if in bouts of happiness, gave me immense pleasure.

In fact, the bumps gave rise to an even greater delight. Here I was on Italian roads, at reasonable speed, the recipient of a whole-body massage, as soothing and refreshing as lying on an air mattress, rocked by the waves' tiny jolts of *joie de vivre*. If these sensations seem far-fetched, I ask for your forbearance. Next time you find yourself in a car that bonds closely with you, on a bumpy stretch of country road (preferably around Pitigliano and after a meal of wild boar), let your imagination have free reign, and perhaps you will discover the soothing, massaging effects of little moguls at speed.

* * *

"No, No, No! Ferrari, rosso, only rosso!"

The object causing offence and needing correction was a spanking clean and exquisitely elegant Ferrari 360 Modena. It was a gorgeous car, but there was one little problem: it was not red, but ice blue metallic and, it should be added, with perfectly matching burgundy interior. A finger-licking vehicle, really, but definitely not rosso.

The time was about three-thirty in the afternoon, and I was really eager to get moving again. I was only going to have this car for one day, so every minute counted. Yet, I had already been sitting there for a good fifteen minutes. By now, I had handed the customs official everything I had: passport, registration, licence, owner's manual. I even offered my miniature, laminated marriage certificate, which he politely refused. Still, he wasn't happy,

and kept circling around my car. One lap, two, then three. Each lap, he did a pit stop to confer with his colleague. The pit stop always took place at the back of my car so I couldn't quite make out what he was doing or saying. Eventually, he came back and commanded me to get out. So I did, and I began to worry. Again, he went to the back of the car, where now there was not only his colleague but also a blood-thirsting German Shepherd. I was wondering if someone had slipped a package of dope under a fender. Finally, he motioned toward the engine compartment where the 360's pride was displayed under glass like a jewel in a display case and in a second it all became clear: would I please be so kind and open the cover so that they could take a closer look?

He conferred with his colleague again, duly noted eight cylinders and finally pronounced his judgement: "Che bella màcchina!" He smiled a passionate smile and his mouth and hand moved to blow a kiss at the car. But then, in evident pain and his head hanging low, repeated his refrain "No, no, no, Ferrari, rosso, only rosso!" At last, he returned the papers to me and gestured that it was ok for me to take my leave. To thank him for his trouble I bolted forward in first gear producing a sound effect that made him give a nod of approval that I saw in my rear view mirror, even as I was pulling quickly away.

This wasn't the first time I'd had this sort of experience. So, I should have cottoned on a lot quicker. Italians are passionate about cars. And they make some of the world's most sensually exhilarating ones to prove it. Think not only Ferrari, but also Maserati, Alfa Romeo, Lancia, Lamborghini and Buggati. Whenever I drive a nice car in Italy – it needn't be a Ferrari as it was on that day – I get pulled over sooner or later by police or customs officials. In most countries, when I'm pulled over, it means I've done wrong. This is invariably humiliating. There is also very little to look forward to except *Schadenfreude* over others being pulled over as well. In Italy, on the other hand, when I get pulled over, there is a good chance that it is simply for the purpose of the officer in charge getting a good look (or to reprimand me for driving a Ferrari that is not rosso). And even if I have committed an offence, I don't despair. I know that the outcome can be debated at length and will depend on the weather, the mood of the officer, the mood of the officer's spouse that morning, my ability to argue and create a believable justification for the offence, the subjectively assessed danger to others created by what I did, and of course, the make and model of my car. The latter, especially if it is an exotic model, can be particularly effective in obtaining compassionate relief. I'm not even apologetic any longer about driving a car that is evidently not a mere form of efficient and clean transport, but instead an unmistakable tool for pleasure. No, I now jump out of my car just as soon as I am stopped, open up the bonnet wide full of pride, all in order to get back on the road again as quickly as possible. Most of the time, that has done the trick.

Shortly after leaving the border crossing, I reached Tirano, a tiny north-Italian town. As I looked at the hustle and bustle and the cars that were on display, I had to conclude that there is more to the Italians' view of cars than just passion. They wear them like fashion. That means two things: there is no accounting for taste, and a hole here or there doesn't matter. It is simply part of what makes you you. And so it is with cars. Just like faded and holed jeans make fashion and a statement of sorts, so an Italian will happily drive a car that sheds paint and has openings unintended by the manufacturer. It certainly won't dent the owner's ego. Cars, like clothes, are an extension of the driver's body. In fact, they are an intimate part of it.

There is also something highly utilitarian about owning a car in Italy. Cars often tend to suffer from terrible neglect: they may smell of edibles – coffee, wine, cheese, tomatoes, fish. Most cars are scratched, have dents and loose bumpers. Observing the scene in Tirano for only a couple of minutes explained why. When Italians park cars they don't rely on vision, but on sound. Once a car is parked, it is kept in place not by the parking brake, but by an engaged gear, 2nd rather than 1st, all the better to be nudged into place by another driver's attempt to squeeze out a spot. Nobody frowns on parking by listening instead of looking. For Italians, it is as natural as shoving together daily-use silverware in a kitchen drawer because a car is as much a means of transporting the owner as a spoon is a means for feeding him.

And so the Italians' attitude toward cars is quite an accurate reflection of their attitude toward life: a curious blend between hot passion and benign neglect.

As I wound my way through Tirano, I suddenly noticed in my rear view mirror a Fiat Cinquecento whose driver was getting closer and closer. Soon, I could only see the driver's head. The rest had seemingly disappeared in my mid-engine compartment, he was that close. I could see not only his head, but also his arms and hands. One was holding a mobile phone into which he talked with pitched excitement, the other was involuntarily waving, the better to express what he was seeing. From what I could gather, he was rather taken by the sight of the 360 and was relaying a detailed description of it to his friend at the other

"... I suddenly noticed a Fiat Cinquecento whose driver was getting **closer and closer.**"

end of the line. How he was steering was not clear.

If I had been anywhere other than in Italy, I would have been worried about the Cinquecento's tailgating, but I had learned long ago that Italians all abide by an unwritten agreement: you pay attention only to what is going on in front and to your side. Never mind what is going on behind you. This is completely different to many other countries where drivers constantly worry about what is happening behind their backs, as it were. That's why it would never occur to an Italian that tailgating somebody else could cause offence. "After all, you're driving forward, are you not? Why look back?" is an Italian's likely justification. It is, however, a nightmare for drivers from most other countries.

Pretty soon the Cinquecento and I came to a pedestrian crossing. That held another lesson in store. The road was two-laned in each direction at this point and the Cinquecento had pulled even with me on my left. At both sides of the crossing, there were people waiting to walk. That made me slow down. Not the Cinquecento, however. He kept going, completely oblivious to the standing pedestrians. I had noticed this before. My teenage sentiments notwithstanding, I had learned that I should let pedestrians cross, especially when there is a marked crossing. For an Italian there is a big difference, however, between a pedestrian that's standing and one that's walking. So long as the pedestrian stands there, the road is open and clear. Once he starts walking into the road, ok, then it's time to stop. And sure enough, the Cinquecento slowed to a halt a little further down the road, where there wasn't even a marked crossing, because some elderly lady had just walked into the road. That was good, too, because it allowed me to catch up with the Cinquecento.

As we were leaving Tirano, he signalled me to pass him, and so I did in a burst of acceleration. That made him smile because, in truth, he'd been waiting for that all along.

After zipping up to 150kmh for a moment, I settled back down to just above a 100. I was fiddling with my stereo for a little while and by the time I looked up, the Cinquecento was back in my engine compartment. I thought these things didn't do more than 85kmh, but there he was, bouncing along this bumpy road in his Cinquecento, revealing without embarrassment its bow-legged wheel camber each time the little thing jumped in the air running over a bump. And guess what? Before I knew it, he had pulled out into the centre lane of this three-lane road. In most other countries, three-lane roads are always nicely separated into sections where first one direction can use the centre lane to pass and then the other. Not so in Italy (or in France, for that matter). No, the centre lane is there for anyone to use. It is a place where the smooth passing of traffic doesn't rely so much on written rules as it relies on the participants' ability to think on their feet. On occasion, this leads to a dent or worse, but it is evident that they prefer individual thinking to submission to rules.

Now, I was doing, as I said, 100kmh. I think he was squeezing out 105, so passing me was going to take a while. At first, this didn't concern me, because there was nothing coming toward us in the centre lane. After what seemed like an eternity, the Cinquecento had pulled even with me. Right about then, an oncoming delivery van decided to pass as well, in that very same centre lane. Now guess what happened? Nothing, nothing at all. All four of us passed each other just fine, because I hugged to my side of the road and so did the being-passed driver on the other side. Also, I slowed down a little to give the Cinquecento room to move back into line, but he didn't make use of it. Relying on me to complete his manoeuvre would have dented his pride, and that would have been entirely unacceptable.

I followed the Cinquecento into the next town where he disappeared down a street which, I swear, had a big "don't enter, one-way street" sign posted on both sides. In Italy, driving is not a public activity like in so many other countries. No, it is, like love, a private activity, an activity of self-expression and, hell, never mind the public. And so, even if they didn't make pizza or pasta, I'd be madly in love with their country.

I might make it in time, if only the road was all **straight** and these **bumps** wouldn't spoil my way.

"Do not go where the path may lead, go instead where there is no path and leave a trail."

And so it does appear that the
lust to drive
is a whole lot more
instinctive
than we might think...

CHAPTER EIGHT

Feeling Free and Alive

"Nothing is worth more than this day." – Johann Wolfgang von Göthe.

There is a road, a month and a time of the day that is special to me. The road is set in the foothills of the Austrian Alps. From the border crossing with Southern Germany, it begins by winding alongside meadows and through dark pine forests up to a narrow hillcrest. The month is May. The meadows are decked out with wild flowers – white snowdrops, yellow and red primroses, blue forget-me-nots, orange dandelion hearts – and adorned with the white-pink coats of blooming fruit trees with black trunks. The time is early morning. The air is sharp and soaked with the dizzying fragrances of spring. The bird song is so lively I can hear it over the rising and falling whir of the engine and the leaves rustling in a light breeze. Arriving at the crest of the hill and before descending to the plain, the beauty of the moment always slows me down. In the distance, the sun is creeping over the mountain ranges, casting its rays across the valley. Down below, dense mist clings to a small lake and spills over onto its shores. Right next to me, tall grass is covered in heavy dew that sparkles in the morning light. Yet, the scenery is not a still life. It changes every minute, revealing new splendour at every turn, because I am neither standing nor walking. Instead, I am covering great distances in no time at all as I descend into the valley following the snaking ribbon of tarmac that hugs the left bank of the glen. As I reach the plain, I dip into the ground-hugging mist, the sun disappears, and before long, my headlights illuminate billowy fog. It feels as though I am driving through cotton wool, dense and lumpy one moment, loose and cuddly the next. A minute later and another two kilometres down the road, at the end of the lake, the sun re-emerges, first as a diffuse, edgeless blot, then with sharp, long, bright rays. Driving on this road, in the morning on a brilliant day in May is, to me, heaven on earth.

It's heaven on earth because it makes me feel boundlessly alive and free. And right here is my link between freedom and driving. I don't know about you, but my daily life is full of constraints. It is rarely simple. And, unless I fight, decisions are made for me. That's why

I treasure anything that makes me feel free. Driving, in one stroke, cuts away constraints, makes life simple and leaves me worry-free and confident to go on adventures. More than anything else, it gives me choices. Driving, at the best of times, turns catacomb into paradise.

* * *

Infinite choice. When I drive, it's me who decides where and when to go, not, for example, the darting whims and surging bladders of thirty-six other travellers on a bus.

Which prompts another thought. It may sound perverse, but to me, one of the greatest pleasures of driving has always been that it lets me stop wherever and whenever I want. I can, whimsically, stop to eat, to drink, to read, to touch, to rest, to smell, to look, to fertilise. It gives me a chance to take in and to absorb whatever piques my curiosity.

But driving makes me feel free not just because I can choose when to stop and when to go, of course, or because it's up to me whether to turn left or right, in the literal sense. It's much more than that. The freedom to choose also empowers me to follow my sixth sense, or that of my wife. When we choose to drive in pursuit of my, or her, sixth sense, it always results in an adventure, most of the time even one we enjoy.

My fondest sixth-sense memory is of a time when my wife and I were looking for a place to have lunch on the way from Geneva to Paris on the A6.

As you know, I live to drive. Driving always comes first. Breathing comes a distant second. Everything else, including necessities such as eating, isn't even on the list. All the years of driving notwithstanding, it is the other way around for my wife. When my wife wants to eat, something must be done about it. Right away. And preferably it is done in a place that she calls "quaint". This automatically ruled out all the restaurants that flanked the highway we were on. They were, in fact, very unquaint.

So, she reached for the map, studied it for a while and then declared,

"Lets get off at Tournus."

"What do you have in mind? Any place in particular?" I asked.

"Nope. But we are bound to find something that's better than what's on offer along the A6," she assured me.

We had no idea where we were going, but that didn't matter because she has an organ that is the very incarnation of her sixth sense: it is her tiny nose, which by then had taken over.

The exit at Tournus dumped us onto the N7.

"Left or right? Please pick a direction," I prompted her.

Her nose twitched for a second and then pointed left. So left it was, and we were going north on the N7. For the moment it didn't look promising at all. The N7 was pretty much dead straight. There weren't any restaurants for miles. But I did not object since I had learned better than to doubt the sensitivity of her nose.

After several minutes we entered Sennecey-le-Grand. A grand, promising name, but nothing caught our attention. The N7, broad and dense with traffic, dominated this town as far as we could tell. This also wasn't quaint. It was still far too close to the humdrum motorway.

> "Only cattle looked up, listlessly **munching** on their **grassy lunch…**"

Then my wife spotted a sign for a road called the D18.

"Let's try that. I just have a feeling…" She intimated that her nose had confided in her that food was "thata way".

The D18 was a winding and bumpy road, with the asphalt patched over and over again. It led us through a grand forest – the Bois du Petit Chorme – and over a narrow stone bridge that crossed the Saône. Within a few more minutes we were in the midst of French farmland. First we drove through Gigny-sur-Saône. There was no restaurant; there weren't even any people. Only cattle looked up, listlessly munching on their grassy lunch with an expression that suggested that we had disturbed their siesta and come dangerously close to being the cause of their indigestion. I wish I *had* something to digest, is all that I could think by then. And onward we drove.

Leaving Gigny, we noted that the next town was St. Germain-du-Plain, about five kilometres away. Several more minutes later – all in all a good forty-five since we had left the A6 – we entered St. Germain full of hope. It was a town of 1,698 souls. We curved around for a while without spotting a restaurant or any people. Once again, we were on the verge of being disappointed. I was very close to asking my dearest what was the matter with her legendary nose when we stumbled upon the town's main square, which was partly covered with giant oak trees. A lonely store seemed to be open. We decided to park near it, in the shade of one of those oaks, to go and ask where we could have lunch. By then anything at all would have been fine, quaint or unquaint.

Just as soon as we got out of our car, a group of school children descended out of nowhere on us. They were full of excitement. We were driving our 911, a car that was obviously rare thereabouts. One of the most confident fellows stepped forward. He beamed at us with bright eyes, and asked, "Can I see the engine?"

"Sure you can, if you can tell us where we can eat!" I shamelessly took advantage of the occasion.

"First open up!" He was not easily deterred.

So I opened up the 911's engine compartment within which sat the perspiring power plant. He took that in for a while, almost crawled into the tiny space, then re-emerged and announced, "C'est un bijou!" Even though I still hadn't eaten, my mood lifted in an instant for I had found a connoisseur. When I was about to engage in a conversation with this young gentleman about the features of my 911's jewel, my wife reminded me what we were here to do.

"Ah, yes, do you know of a place where we can eat?" I asked him again.

"Of course, just down this way for about a kilometre and a half, on the left-hand side as you leave town. You can't miss it," he explained. "And thanks for the good look at the engine. It really is a beauty, that thing of yours."

While I was still wondering what precisely he meant, my wife's nose twitched furiously again. Within about a minute we spotted the place he must have meant. It was called Chez CatPat and didn't look like much. Before it were parked pick-up trucks and farm implements with wheels. It certainly didn't look quaint in the sense that my wife uses the term: cosy, rustic, gemütlich. No, it was none of that.

We parked our car among the tractors. It looked horribly out of place, but not nearly as out of place as ourselves when we stepped into the restaurant through the open door. The boisterous laughter and clanking of dishes and glasses stopped in an instant. We were two over-dressed Martians who had fallen from the sky, which was about to cave in on the heads of a group of startled, blue-overalled, French earthlings. Apparently, visitors were rare in St. Germain-du-Plain.

We feared we were in for a sore disappointment after having spent almost an hour in search of lunch. But nothing could have been further from the truth. We ended up having one of the best lunch-time experiences ever. We ate a sumptuous meal: potato salad to start, then a soup, a main course of chicken Provençale, an Ile Flottante as dessert, bread, a selection of fine cheeses, a large bottle of water and an equally large bottle of red wine to match (which my wife reminded me I could only have a sip of) – all of it for Euro 30. When the erstwhile suspicious locals noticed that we ate their cuisine with gusto, they instantly made us feel at home. Chez CatPat really ended up feeling like home when Catherine, the owner, explained the play of words in her restaurant's name. Her name was Catherine; her husband's Patrick. "Plus", she went on, "we have a little dog, a quattres pattes, which, if you say it quickly in French, sounds like CatPat."

What an unforgettable discovery we had made! Not through careful planning or meticulously following directions. No, simply by letting ourselves be guided by the freedom of choice that comes with driving and the sensitivity of my wife's nose.

* * *

If driving were only about the freedom to choose, it'd already top my list of pleasurable activities. But what really sets it apart is that it has the power to make life simple, remove all constraints and open up space.

There was no better example of that than when I went for the first time to Australia for a Christmas holiday. It was 7:30pm on the day before Christmas Eve. That evening, I dropped, perspiring and panting, into a seat on Hong Kong's Airport Express. The train was spilling over with people leaving the territory, on their way to anywhere, for the destination

did not seem to matter. What mattered most was that one went elsewhere, for elsewhere there would be more space than in Hong Kong which is among the most densely populated areas in the world. (Sections of it, it is hard to imagine, are home to over fifty thousand busy bodies per square kilometre.)

On my way to the airport and then to my departure gate for flight CX171 to Perth, I tried, I tried really hard to recall what space felt like, what the statistic of 2.5 inhabitants per square kilometre in all of Australia (and less in Western Australia, "WA") meant for breathing. It was difficult, and I gave up, because the reality for the moment meant making my way first through a heaving mass of people at the airport and then squeezing into my economy class seat whose limited space was further narrowed by the spill-over of co-travellers. Do they pay more? Ten dollars for every trespassing pound?

My destination was not Perth, in fact, but a remote vineyard in Margaret River, four hours' drive south of Perth. My wife was there already. Yet my holiday, my liberation into space, would begin, not with arriving in Margaret River, but the moment I landed and climbed into my rental car. I was filled to the brim with anticipation and tried to make time pass quickly with dinner, a movie and sleep. But sleep didn't come. The harder I tried, the further it receded. And the more I thought about open space, the more claustrophobic my flight felt. I longed for the landing and driving south.

There was no queue at customs. I rushed to the rental car counter and almost ran to the car park. I threw in my luggage. Nothing seemed to matter; nothing except my getting on the road.

It was shortly before sunrise. The air was transparent and crisp, but promising heat. I had arrived in the Australian summer. When I exited the parking lot, there was hardly a car in sight. I found my way to the highway, scrolled down the window, put my arm on the windowsill, accelerated into the morning and felt free in an instant.

Once out of the metropolitan area and on the way to wine country, I had three hours of open roads ahead of me, all laid out among the rugged beauty of WA – arid, yet lush with Jarrah and Karri trees and WA's state emblem, red and green kangaroo paws. All tiredness had vanished. My mind was full of excitement over the conquering of space and the escape from constraint, and my skin prickled because the air brushed across my arm at a hundred kilometres an hour. It was an overpoweringly tactile experience, so powerful that it made me aware of having skin, of having an arm.

(Many years later I would read Oliver Sacks' *The Man Who Mistook his Wife for a Hat* in which he tells the story of a young lady, "the disembodied lady", who lost the ability to sense her body. "There are brief, partial reprieves, when her skin is stimulated," he wrote. "She goes out when she can, she loves open cars, where she can feel the wind on her body and face. 'It's wonderful', she says, 'I feel the wind on my arms and face, and then I know, faintly, I have arms and a face. It's not the real thing, but it's something – it lifts the horrible, dead veil for a while.'")

The air on my skin cooled my entire body. And it made the hair on my furry arm dance and shimmer in the colours of the rainbow. All along, I was entertained by that miniature performance. On occasion, I even raised my arm to smell it because there is a special smell to air-brushed, dry skin.

Little did I know that I would pay a steep price for my indulgence: the following day I would be nursing a severe sunburn on my right arm that went from my knuckles to two inches below my shoulder, interrupted only by a narrow ribbon with a circular top where my watch had rested. I would be pink, in pain and grumpy. When I mentioned it to my wife she gave me one of those looks that said it all – "if only husbands would listen to wives…" – because only the day before she had reminded me that when in Australia, you must, before going out, "slip, slop, slap": slip on your sunnies, slop on some sun screen, slap on your hat. I let my head hang low in contrition.

But driving in the wind that day was glorious since I had no inkling of the sunburn or the ridicule to come. Instead, it reminded me of how much I love being exposed to the elements, sun, wind and water, be it as rain or as snow. Lest you get the wrong impression, I am no Scot or Livingstone. These are people whom I admire, but their aspirations aren't mine. For me, even camping carries outdoor adventure too far. I am instead a bucket seat adventurer. I like being exposed to the elements the way I am in a car. Inside the cabin and under glass, the sun feels hotter than it ever does out in the open. Feeling powerful rain while driving is always refreshing. When the rain whips against the car and almost forces the wipers to a halt, when the wipers clear oceans from the windscreen, all I need to do in order to feel the perfect level of exposure to the element that is water, is to open the window a tiny bit and sense the fine spray of water droplets on my skin. Or take snow. I freeze when the temperature drops below ten degrees Celsius, I really do. (Scot's party

"In winter landscape that is frozen solid,
I feel my **perceptiveness** heightened
and at **one** with the **world**…"

travelling for three months at minus fifty degrees Celsius and below in utter darkness is completely beyond my comprehension.) But driving in a snow storm with my high beams on to illuminate the furious dancing of snow flakes as, with all their weightless might, they avoid settling on the ground, now that, to me, is an exhilarating immersion into the freezing world of impenetrable snow. When I experience the elements in this way, I feel my perceptiveness heightened and at one with the world.

As I drove under the perspiring sun and the breathing wind, I found that my perceptiveness was heightened further still by the very fact of moving at speed. Focusing my eyes on the near-by instead of the horizon, shrank distances, and "over there" became "right here" in less time than I could form impressions. Why did it sharpen my senses? Why did it feel so liberating? Because, even at the moderate 100kmh at which I was driving, I was moving faster than I could ever be carried by my own legs. I suppose I can get close to this sensation of speed when I do a hundred meter dash. When I run at top speed completely out of breath with my heart pounding and my muscles straining, then I do feel a rush of speed, but I am actually too exhausted to take full notice. Driving down south on the highway, on the other hand, my heart beat pretty much as if I was at rest, with my blood pressure at 105 over 65 – well, maybe a bit higher. Yet, my senses were as keen and ticklish as if I were intoxicated. To me, this epitomised the very essence of driving pleasure: I could observe life and participate in it, both at the same time.

After driving south for about two hours, first past Rockingham, and then by Mundarah's Peel Inlet, which was lined with beach holiday homes, I wanted to confirm my bearings. By then I felt completely relaxed, so I made a point of turning off the engine and leisurely rolling to a halt. I lightly tugged on the steering wheel to veer from the hot tarmac onto the gravely parking area by the road. First two wheels, then all four touched the gravel with that unmistakable, lively crunching sound that rubber makes on pebble stones. Without the engine running, I could almost hear the tyres making contact, moulding themselves to the surface and then spewing out each pebble. A faint dust cloud appeared in my rear view mirrors, but the wind dispersed it before it had time to form. And then my car stopped moving. There was silence, complete silence, except for the sounds of the Australian bush.

After a minute, I got out, stretched and spread out the map on my car's bonnet. With my eyes squinting in the sun, I searched for where I was. When I had located my position, I smiled. As far as the rest of the world was concerned, I was nowhere. Perth, the nearest large city, was already three hours away in the north. And Perth itself is the remotest large city on Earth. So, being nowhere was just about right. I smiled because in all other circumstances being "nowhere" would mean that the exhilarating sense of freedom would be tempered – at least for me, the bucket seat adventurer – by an unmistakable feeling of concern. But not in my car. In my car, I could do things that I never, ever could without it. I could be nowhere and yet so close to anywhere. So, at that moment, as I was leaning back against the car and looking up into the bluest of all skies and the whitest of all suns in the

middle of nowhere, the world was an opalescent pearl in the palm of my hand.

But soon I wanted to get going again, to continue my journey on the highway leading south. Where I was driving, there was nothing but flatness, no mountains to curb space. Weatherboard houses, blackboy trees that looked like low fountains frozen in time, and bottlebrush bushes marked the highest elevation. At that time of day, the roads were almost empty, straight and without interruptions. Traffic lights were few and fewer still the cars that were joining or departing the loose stream of traffic. All the obstacles of my daily life leading up to when I had boarded the Hong Kong Airport Express train fourteen hours earlier had disappeared, completely. Life had become so simple. Even the imaginary puddles of water on the glistening road made way for me, one by one, as I approached them. Nothing could feel as soothingly antipodal to Hong Kong as driving on that open road.

I don't recall when morning turned into day. The air above the road began to shimmer. The cicadas woke up, began to scratch and chime into the soft sounds of driving into open space. Their whir slowly rose and subsided. The engine hummed as it ploughed through thick and thicker air and the tyres whizzed on the black road surface. The landscape, too, lacked limiting edges. The earth was rusty-brown and the bushes dull green; they blurred one into the other. There was nothing in the landscape that distracted or demanded focus. Only the dark blue of the sky drew my attention, and it was remarkable for nothing but its infinity. Driving there drew my mind into the open spaces that made me feel free and alive.

EPILOGUE

"The world is round and the place which may seem like the end
may also be only the beginning."
— Ivy Baker Priest.

Throughout the years, I've never stopped loving driving, nor have I managed to quench my thirst for it. Recently, I drove seventeen thousand kilometres on an extended trip to Europe and the U.K. in the course of about six weeks. When I returned home, my wife was pretty certain that that must have done the trick.

"You must be sick of driving by now, surely!"

She couldn't have been more wrong.

GET IN TOUCH

READERS

Can you relate to what you've read and seen? Enjoyed part or all of it? Or do you think there is a whole lot more to the pleasures of driving? Want to be in touch with others who love being on the road? Have a strong opinion about the world's most beautiful roads? Or are you thinking about planning a driving holiday with your friends or family?

For all this and more, make **www.ontheroadeditions.com** *your next destination. And if you register, too, I'll remember to send you future on-the-road editions at a substantial discount.*

TRAVEL AND MOTORING WRITERS

Have you had wonderful and memorable on-the-road adventures and experiences? Do you have on-the-road stories to tell? Do you want to see them published? I am looking for travel and motoring writers who are interested in creating with me future on-the-road editions.

You can get in touch with me at: **peter@ontheroadeditions.com**

PHOTOGRAPHERS AND ILLUSTRATORS

Do you have a library of amazing and stunning on-the-road photographs or illustrations? If you are interested in having your beautiful photographs or illustrations published, or if you want to contribute to future on-the-road editions, I would love to hear from you.

You can get in touch with me at: **peter@ontheroadeditions.com**

ACKNOWLEDGEMENTS

Before I began working on *On the Road,* whenever I read a non-fiction book and glanced over the acknowledgement section, I invariably wondered: why is it that writers say thanks to so many people? Didn't they do any work themselves?

Never, ever will I wonder again.

First I would like to thank an admirable lady by the name of Chris Sawyer. What makes her special is this: not only did she not faint when she saw the first draft of my manuscript, she actually managed to see – heavens knows how! – the seeds of something vaguely worthwhile. So she went on to tell me everything that was bad – a lot – but also the few bits that were promising. She continued to coax and coach and, well, the manuscript turned into what it is today. Alas Chris could not work miracles. Therefore, the responsibility for all the errors and oddities that remain is mine and mine alone.

I also needed and received a lot of help in collecting the photographs at the lowest possible expense. It is a story worth telling in brief. I began by working my network. At first I was amazed that everyone I approached seemed to know exactly what I was after. They all assured me that they could easily help because they said to themselves: "He says he's writing a book about driving, but surely what he means is 'a book about cars'". As a result, the first photos I was shown were invariably about stationary cars, under studio light, and, with bad luck, scantily clad ladies draped across them. When this repeated itself five or six times, it became painfully clear that while there are a gazillion photos about cars, there are very, very few about driving. For example, when I visited one manufacturer's archive, I moused through 10,000 digital images in one day to wind up with ...precisely...*one* that fit. But at least I *did* find one. That is why I needed a tremendously sympathetic and attentive ear behind every door on which I knocked. While it usually took some time for my interlocutors to "get it", most who eventually did, worked hard, even tirelessly, to help me. And so, thanks to the help of all those who "got it" – "ah, I see, a book about driving, not cars" – I ended up with what could just be the world's largest and most inspiring collection of photographs about the joys of being on the road.

Without further ado, I am immensely grateful to those who helped me find, sponsored, or donated photographs: Hans Hoegstedt of Alfa Romeo; Barbara Prince of Aston Martin; Neil Murray of the Aston Martin Heritage Trust; Gordon Choy and Paul Zimmerman of Aston Martin Hong Kong; Lothar Franz of Audi AG; Urs Killer and Christian Klainguti of the Austin Healey Club Switzerland; Leonore Hamann, Chris Koenders, Mr. Reinhardt, Ms. Standfuss and Sabine Zehetner of BMW AG; Andy Noble and David Wakefield of Caterham Cars; Tony Churly of 'Stelvio or Bust'; Tobias Reich of DaimlerChrysler; Tim Damon; David Burgess and Rob Esser of David Esser.com; Antonio Ghini, Stefania Martinelli, Silvia Pini and Silvio Vigato of Ferrari-Maserati; Sudhir Saday of Ford; Anders Clausager, Jonathan Griffiths, Karam Ram, Simon Roebuck and Cecile Simon-Chapotier of Jaguar; Chris King; Paul Jones and Sonia Petrazzi of La Presse; Ivan Lobbia, Luca de

Meo and Edith Wassenaar of Lancia; James Andrew of Land Rover; Peter Lenhardt; Laurence Jourdain, Fiona Pattiselano and Sylvie Renouard of Lexus Europe Marketing; Alastair Florance of Lotus; Peter Fritz of M.L. Gaukler Werbeagentur; Dan McNally; Stefan Brommer of Mercedes Benz; Dagmar Bardelmeier and Andreas Pichler of the MG Interessengemeinschaft Scuderia Froschenteich; Chacky Ip of South China Media; Walter Laimer and Gert Pichler of Nostalgic; Silvana Appendino and Anna Artigiani of Pininfarina; Tariq Boutaleb, Didier Richard, Frédéric Schulz, and Claude Teissier of PSA Peugeot Citroën; Willie Von Recklinghausen; Klaus Schnitzer; Hermann Dinklage, Peter Wafzig and Michael Mittler of smart Club Germany; Colleen Falken, Arthur Kipferler and Johan Verhezen of Toyota Europe Marketing; Andrew Cullis, Collette Dunkley and Joanne Harrison-Gross of Opel and Vauxhall; Jens Bobsien, Dr. Dirk Schlinkert, Matthias Stenzel and Hardy Wiesner of Volkswagen.

A few people deserve special mention and thanks; without them *On the Road* would not be what it is: there is Jeff Bishop, who did not mind being tracked down by a detective bureau and then went out of his way to get me the "jumping Fiat 500" photo; there are Lapo Elkann, Matthew Kentridge, and Richard Witts who gave advice or provided support just when it was needed; there are Hermann Becker, Alessandro Furfaro, and Sebastian Piëch who, with a few phone calls and emails, connected me with numerous people who then went on to find and sponsor photos for me; Andrew Windebank of the Hong Kong Automobile Association who unfailingly provided support, including the use of his Caterham 7 for a photo shoot; Chris and Chiaki Fjelddahl and their children as well as Marie Burns who are immortalised in the "family drive" shot; and last, but certainly not least, Ron Yue, who shot some awesome photographs.

I also want to thank my friends and relatives for the support they've given me during the development of *On the Road*: how can one possibly remain a friend to anyone who keeps talking about nothing but driving and writing his darn book for nigh on two years? Somehow they remained friends. (My relatives had no choice but to stay my relatives; but I thank them anyway for still talking to me.) My friends and relatives lent an ear or their car or both, put me up at their home, provided me stories to tell, read early drafts and were bold enough to make comments, made invaluable introductions or spoke encouraging words when I really needed them... Joanna Anthony; Jennifer Carver; Andrew Cheung; Ian Beck; Ken Deen; Martin Fairbairn; Douglas Gautier; Ian Henry; Alex Key; Geoff King; Swee-Yen Koong and Finian Koong; Jacinta Sutton and Andy Lake; Rodney Hanratty and Andrew and John Lam-Po-Tang; Lester Lim; Joe Mueller; Erland Sternby and Jennifer Rodriguez; James, Margaret and Margaret Ma Stuart; Donald Sutherland; Jo Soo and Mike Tang; Larry Ng and Valerie Tham; Hardy Tschofen; Michael Warszawski; and Anne Troulay and Wuimin Wong.

I also want to express my gratitude to my mom Fridl. Not only did she merrily raise a car- and speed-crazed youngster who dented her car as often as her hopes that I would turn into a worthwhile individual, but she actually provided unfailing support and encouragement for my racing and driving desires even when she must have felt an irresistible urge to question my choices.

And then there is my wife to whom I have been nothing but a series of challenges, most of them seemingly insurmountable, surely. And yet, time and again, she has stood by me, loving me, allowing me to be myself and to pursue the dream of bringing *On the Road* to life.

END NOTES

OPENING POEM

1. The opening poem has been adapted from the following:

Dance as though no one is watching you,
Love as though you have never been hurt before,
Sing as though no one can hear you,
Live as though heaven is on earth.

This prayer's source is unknown.

CHAPTER TWO

2. Arthur Drexler, curator of architecture at the museum of modern arts in the 1950s, coined the phrase "Art in Motion" on the occasion of Pininfarina's then-latest automotive creation, the Cisitalia 202, being taken into the museum's permanent collection.

3. "Life is not a journey to the grave with the intention of arriving safely in a pretty and well-preserved body, but rather to skid in broadside, thoroughly used up, totally worn out and loudly proclaiming: 'Wow, what a ride!'" I received this quote from a friend who could not trace its source. If you know who first said it, please let me know. I would like to give credit.

CHAPTER THREE

4. The idea that "rushing along at high and higher speed had become not an affirmation of life, but a form of death" is an adaptation of a section in *The Meaning of Happiness* by Alan Watts, Harper, New York, 1940.

5. The idea that we might enjoy dancing to music so much because our entire body resonates to its tune is adapted from *Music, The Brain and Ecstasy*, by Robert Jourdain, Quill, 2002.

CHAPTER FIVE

6. The image of geese taking flight is adapted from "Geese take flight perfectly at V's" by Doug O'Harra, Anchorage Daily News, October 25, 2000.

CHAPTER SIX

7. With reference to the passing manoeuvre described on page 115, I must say that hesitation is not a good idea when passing other cars. However, getting back in your own lane *is* a very good idea if and when on-coming traffic appears. There is nothing more inappropriate or dangerous than to remain in the passing lane when one has underestimated the distance one requires to pass. Better to feel embarrassed than to be dead.

8. To "wedel": a style of skiing in which a skier rhythmically swings the rear of the skis from side to side while following the fall line, Merriam Webster, Online Edition, www.w-m.com.

9. The quote on page 139 is anonymous according to *The Penguin Dictionary of Modern Humorous Quotations*.

CHAPTER SEVEN

10. The idea that "our experiences of a place are most enjoyable if we're not faced with the additional challenge of having to be there" is adapted from *The Art of Travel*, Alain de Botton, Penguin, p. 20 and p. 23.

11. The German fines for various insults is taken from http://www.fun-fahrschule-ff.de/text/bel.html.

12. Schadenfreude is often translated as "malicious joy". But that makes it sound as if German-speaking people take delight in other people's misfortune. The reality is more subtle. Schadenfreude means taking delight in somebody else's obviously deserved misfortune, such as being pulled over by the police for speeding.

13. The Italians are often accused of being the most murderous on roads. However, researching statistics from the EU and Switzerland in 2001, I found that Italy has by no means the highest annual road death toll as a percentage of registered vehicles. Portugal is the leader. Italy is about as safe (or unsafe) as Denmark and Austria, but, it must be said, not as safe as Switzerland or the UK.

14. While I have seen plenty of Italians driving down one-way streets, in the instance described on page 156, a closer look revealed that the restriction applied to a different time of day.

15. The quote on page 162 is by Ralph Waldo Emerson.

CHAPTER EIGHT

16. The story about the "disembodied lady" comes from *The Man Who Mistook his Wife for a Hat*, Oliver Sacks, Picador, 1986, page 51.

CREDITS

PHOTO CREDITS

The photographs featured in *On the Road* have been drawn from many different sources: amateur and professional photographers, automobile manufacturers and photo agencies. I would like to thank them all for their kind permission to reproduce their photographs in *On the Road*.

Aston Martin Heritage Trust: 92 - Louis Klementaski

Audi AG: 133 - Helmut Binder

BMW AG: 14, 50, 70

Car Plus Magazine / South China Media: 142 - Ringo Ng K.H.

Corbis: ii - Joe Bator; 46 - Blake Woken; 55 - Joseph Sohm; 60 - Craig Aurness; 64 - David Stoecklein; 68 - Ron Watts; 86 - Martyn Goddard; 136 - Mark Peterson; 138 - Chuck Savage; 175 - Robert Landau; 186 - Owaki Kulla

Daimler Chrysler AG Stuttgart: 72

Hermann Dinklage: vi

Ferrari SpA: 17 - LaPresse / Noris; 106 – LaPresse; 153 - Frank Orel; 180 - LaPresse / Noris

Fiat Auto SpA Brand Lancia: 150 - Terry Deroy Gruber

Chris Fjelddahl: 76

Derek Gardner: Back Cover

Getty Images: Front Cover - Brendan Byrne; v - Walter Bibikow; 5 - Alvis Upitis; 6 - Angello Cavalli; 11 - Arnulf Husno; 13 - National Geographic / Raymond K. Gehman; 59 - Jeremy Woodhouse; 74 - Allan R. Moller; 88 - Emma Lee; 105 - Jorg Greuel; 114 - Loraine Wilson; 117 - Thierry Dosogne; 120 - Siegfried Layda; 126 - Peter Hendrie; 129 - Vince Streano; 157 - Joe Cornish; 158 - Will & Deni McIntyre; 164 - Ryan McVay; 170 - Digital Vision; 172 - Terie Rakke; 176 - Mitchell Funk

Goodshoot: 96

John Hallett: 131

Index Stock: 32 - Bud Freund; 178 - Jim Vitali

Jaguar Cars Ltd: 42 - Pete Davies

Angie Koong: Back-cover gatefold

Land Rover Ltd: 160

Lexus Division Europe: 149 - Daniel Hartz

Group Lotus Plc: 2, 66 - Jason Parnell and Jarowan Power

Maserati SpA: 53 - LaPresse / Noris

Rudolf Menzi: 18 - Rudolf Menzi

MG Interessengemeinschaft Scuderia Froschenteich / Dagmar Bardelmeier: 41, 100, 134, 135, 182

NASA: 191

Nostalgic: 37 - Gert Pichler; 112 - Helmut Thoma

Pininfarina SpA: 25 - W. S. Eberle

Peter Schindler: 26, 78

Klaus Schnitzer: 84

Source Unknown: 39 (please contact the publisher)

Toyota Motors Europe: 20 - Tim Damon; 48 - Willie Von Recklinghausen; 184

Vauxhall Ltd: 188 - Dan McNally

Volkswagen AG: 162, 166

Peter Wafzig: 83, 192

Ron Yue: 22, 29, 140

ILLUSTRATION CREDIT

I would like to express my thanks as well to Emilio Rivera III for his illustrations, illustrations that bring unforgettable moments to life.

...And if, per chance, one day we felt that on earth there were no more roads left to discover, it needn't mean the end of the journey...

Copyright Notice

ON THE ROAD

First published in 2005 by On the Road Editions Limited, 11D London Court, 41 Conduit Road, Hong Kong.

www.ontheroadeditions.com

Illustrations: Emilio Rivera III
Production manager: Aliena Lai
Printed in Hong Kong

eight
publishing

ISBN-988-98256-1-9

Design and Production by Eight Publishing Ltd